Step-by-Step

WOODWORK PROJECTS

Step-by-Step
WOODWORK
PROJECTS

G J ENGELBRECHT

PHOTOGRAPHY BY JUAN ESPI
ILLUSTRATIONS BY CLARENCE CLARKE

NEW
HOLLAND

First published in 1995 by
New Holland (Publishers) Ltd
London • Cape Town • Sydney • Singapore

24 Nutford Place,
London W1H 6DQ
United Kingdom

80 McKenzie Street,
Cape Town 8001
South Africa

3/2 Aquatic Drive,
Frenchs Forest, NSW 2086
Australia

Reprinted 1995, 1996 and 1997

ISBN 1 85368 340 X (hb)
ISBN 1 85368 341 8 (pb)

Editors: Sandie Vahl and Coral Walker
Project coordinator: Cherie Hawes
Designer: Peter Bosman
Cover designer: Jenny Frost and Peter Bosman
Illustrator: Clarence Clarke
Indexer and proofreader: Hilda Hermann

Typesetting by Dierdre Geldenhuys,Struik DTP
Reproduction by Unifoto (Pty) Ltd
Printed and bound in Malaysia by Times Offset (M) Sdn Bhd

CONTENTS

INTRODUCTION 7

PROJECTS
Key rack 20
Hall stand 22
Hall table with drawers 26
Telephone table 29
Magazine rack 32
Coffee table 34
Music centre cabinet 37
Wall cabinet 40
Dining-room table 44
Cocktail cabinet/serving trolley 47
Display cabinet 52
Vegetable cutting board 55
Bathroom cabinet 57
Towel rack 60
Mirror frame 63
Double-bed base 65
Dressing table 67
Child's bed/desk unit 70
Bookrack 73
Bookcase 75
Filing unit 78
Sewing centre 80
Tool chest 84
Carpenter's workbench 88

LIST OF SUPPLIERS 93

GLOSSARY 94

FURTHER READING 95

INDEX 96

INTRODUCTION

The do-it-yourself concept is as old as the existence of man. However, since the days when people made household articles because it was a practical necessity, the emphasis has shifted, and today woodwork is enjoyed as a recreational activity that is both functional and creative. Do-it-yourself enthusiasts can express their creativity while escaping from the humdrum routine and stresses of everyday life, and derive pleasure from making something useful. Many a woodwork hobbyist can attest to the great sense of accomplishment that making a piece of furniture brings – right from the time the piece begins to take shape until the proud moment when the perfectly finished article takes its place in the home.

Although wood is not necessarily cheap, you can save a great deal of money by making your own furniture. You will probably find that you can afford to and be inspired to make a piece you would not normally consider purchasing.

Do-it-yourself projects require specific knowledge and skills. The purpose of this book is to give you the basic information required before you begin, and then lead you step-by-step through each project. Obviously, the secret of do-it-yourself is to get it right and produce a final product which you are proud of. The satisfaction you will derive from achieving this aim is your ultimate reward. I hope that this book will assist you in experiencing that feeling of achievement.

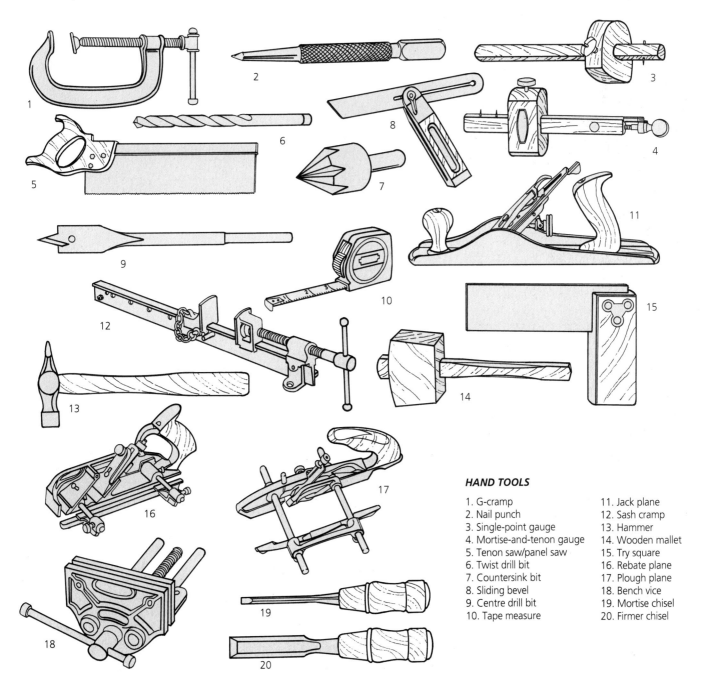

HAND TOOLS

1. G-cramp	11. Jack plane
2. Nail punch	12. Sash cramp
3. Single-point gauge	13. Hammer
4. Mortise-and-tenon gauge	14. Wooden mallet
5. Tenon saw/panel saw	15. Try square
6. Twist drill bit	16. Rebate plane
7. Countersink bit	17. Plough plane
8. Sliding bevel	18. Bench vice
9. Centre drill bit	19. Mortise chisel
10. Tape measure	20. Firmer chisel

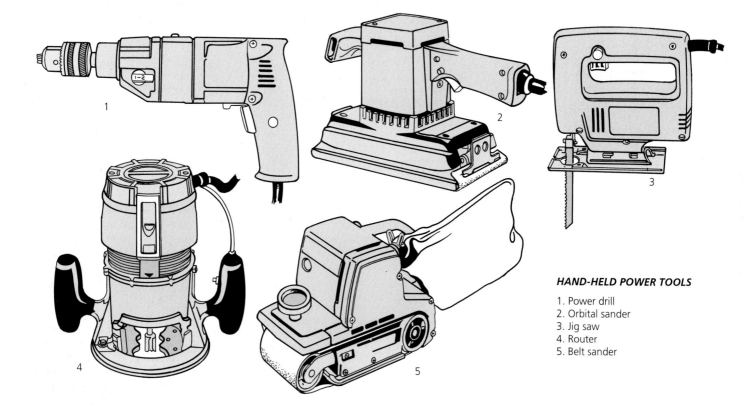

HAND-HELD POWER TOOLS

1. Power drill
2. Orbital sander
3. Jig saw
4. Router
5. Belt sander

TOOLS AND TECHNIQUES

This book offers a range of more than 20 practical projects for making various items of furniture for your home. In many of the projects, alternative shapes or plans are given to extend the scope of your choice so that you can adapt them to suit your own taste and style.

First of all we discuss the basic tools that you will require (hand tools, hand-held power tools and machine tools), some basic materials, and the construction techniques that you will need to know to complete the projects. Study this section, since the tools and/or construction techniques will be referred to in the projects. A list of materials, followed by illustrated step-by-step instructions on how to make the article, is given for each project.

TOOLS

Most of the basic procedures in woodwork, such as preparing the wood, measuring and marking-off joints, shaping, constructing and assembling the project, can be done with hand tools. A list of essential hand tools is found on this page, and certain are illustrated on page 7. The tools are arranged according to the functions they perform. Power and machine tools do simplify some tasks, however, and the different types and their uses are also discussed. (*See also* Woodturning tools and their functions, pages 17-18).

Preparation of wood (planing to size or dressing)
* jack plane
* marking gauge
* try square
* tape measure or ruler

Measuring joints and shaping
* ruler or tape measure
* single-point gauge
* mortise-and-tenon gauge (double-point gauge)
* pencil compass
* sliding bevel or dovetail plate

Joints, mouldings and construction
* set of firmer chisels – 6 mm (¼ in), 9 mm (⅜ in), 12 mm (½ in), 25 mm (1 in)
* 6 mm (¼ in) mortise chisel (for cutting mortises)
* bench saw (either panel or dovetail)
* wooden mallet (to drive chisels)
* set of drill bits (straight shank, high-speed, steel twist drills) – 3 mm (⅛ in), 6 mm (¼ in)
* centre bits to drill larger holes
* sash cramps or T-bar cramps
* G-cramps (or C-clamps)
* workbench with bench vice (to secure wooden boards while working)
* small metal hammer
* nail punch to countersink nails
* countersink bit to countersink screw heads
* plough plane to cut grooves
* rebate plane to cut rebates

HAND-HELD POWER TOOLS

The five most important hand-held power tools required to make the articles in this book are a power drill, a jig saw, an orbital sander, a router and a belt sander.

Power drill You will find a drill indispensable for constructing most of the furniture featured in the following pages. This tool will be used for drilling holes to insert screws, attaching door and drawer handles, shaping keyholes and a variety of other tasks. Remember that many kinds of drill bits and countersinks can only be used with power drills.

Special attachments are available for some kinds of drills, for example for planing and fretting, so that you don't have to purchase separate power tools for these tasks. For heavy-duty work, however, a self-contained machine, such as an orbital sander, is better than the kind that is attached to a drill.

Jig saw For the projects in this book, a jig saw can be used very effectively for sawing decorative curves or patterns. You can also use it to saw out certain joints, such as the dovetails for dovetail joints. A jig saw is also a very handy tool when you have to saw large sheets of plywood for the backs of cabinets. Several kinds of blade are available, for example for sawing hard or soft wood.

Sawing a curve with a jig saw

Moulding an edge with a router

A leg being turned on a lathe

Orbital sander An orbital sander is particularly useful for medium and fine sanding. The size of the base plate varies from one-third of a sheet to half a sheet of sandpaper. With some of the smaller sanders, the sanding pads are attached to the base with Velcro, but normally the sanding paper is secured with clips. This kind of sander makes the finishing process considerably easier, although the final sanding should be done by hand – still the best finishing method.

Belt sander This kind of sander is used mainly for rough sanding, for example to smooth glued-up table tops or the sides of cabinets. Although fine to rough belts are available for these sanders, the fine belts can leave unsightly marks which then have to be removed with an orbital sander.

Different makes have belts in various lengths, while widths ranging from 75 mm (3 in) to 100 mm (4 in) are available.

Belt sanders collect sanding dust in a dust bag. You can mix this dust with a sanding sealer to fill up small holes. This is a very effective way of repairing sanded wood with a matching filler.

A belt sander is used for rough sanding

Router A router is used to cut and shape edges (for tables), mouldings and grooves (for housing joints). Bits in various shapes are available, as well as accessories for making dovetail joints (for example, for drawer construction).

Technical specifications Consult your dealer about the technical specifications of these five power tools. Compare the features of the different makes, and decide which tools will best suit your purposes and which you can afford. Your dealer will be able to advise you on maintenance and, of particular importance, how to use the tools safely.

MACHINE TOOLS
Machine tools are very expensive and it is possible to make do without them. They do, however, help to make any DIY job considerably easier, since you can saw and plane wood to measure and make joints quickly and accurately.

The most useful basic machine tools are a lathe, a circular saw, a band saw, a surface planer, a drill press and a thicknesser. These machines can be purchased as purpose-built units or in combination, with up to five essential functions (and more) in one compact machine. This is usually a cheaper option than buying the tools individually. A combination machine does require more discipline and planning, however, as only one or two functions can be used at a time. As an alternative, these machines can usually be hired from your nearest plant hire centre.

Lathe Lathes are used to shape chair, table and cabinet legs by turning the wood. Shaping is done by means of special tools or chisels. This process is clearly explained in the section on 'Woodturning tools and their functions' on pages 17-18.

The principal difference between the various models lies in the length and diameter of the legs that can be turned on them. Some more expensive lathes are equipped with a copier, which facilitates turning a number of identical legs. Essentially, your lathe should be able to turn a leg with a length of at least 750 mm (2 ft 5½ in). Longer items such as the stiles of bed posts, are usually turned in sections and then joined with dowels.

Circular saw This saw is used primarily for ripping wide boards into smaller parts and for sawing boards lengthways. It can also be used to saw the tenons for mortise-and-tenon joints, and the grooves for housing joints.

There are two main types on the market: a cabinet and a radial saw. Ripping is easier with the cabinet type, while a radial saw is more effective for cross-grain sawing and for cutting grooves. Both can be used for other tasks. A whole range of accessories (such as sanding drums) is available for the radial saw.

When long sheets of wood, for example chipboard, have to be sawn and one person is handling the job, it is better to use a radial saw, since the wood remains stationary and does not have to be handled.

Cross-cutting a specific length

Band saw This saw is used primarily for sawing curves and irregular shapes. It can also be used to saw the parts of joints, such as dovetails for dovetail joints and tenons for mortise-and-tenon joints.

The capability of this saw is restricted by the width and thickness of the board or beam that can be fed through it. Different blade widths, ranging from 6 mm (¼ in) to 19 mm (¾ in), can be mounted on it, and the narrower the blade, the smaller the circumference of the circle or the curve that can be sawn.

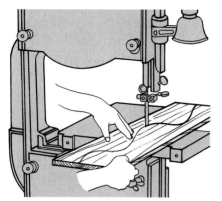

Sawing a curve on a band saw (see page 9)

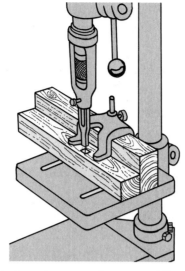

Mortise-and-tenon attachment on a drill press

Planing wood on a surface planer

Surface planer A surface planer is used to smooth and true-up the faces and edges of a board. Some surface planers can be used for planing rebates, while others can plane diagonally (for example 45°) for mitred joints.

Surface planers are used primarily for trueing-up the edges of boards when a butt joint is required (when glueing together table tops). When a beam has to be planed square, two adjoining sides are first planed straight and true on the surface planer, and then the opposite sides are planed true and to size on a thicknesser.

Thicknesser As its name indicates, a thicknesser is used for planing boards to thickness, and in the case of narrow beams, to width. This machine is usually available in combination with a surface planer, and is only restricted by the width of the boards it can plane.

Drill press A drill press drills holes accurately and quickly. It ensures that holes are drilled completely square (at 90°) to the surface, which is important when a carcass is secured with wooden dowels. The best feature of this machine is that, with the right accessories, you can use it to make tenons for all mortise-and-tenon joints,

making it, in effect, the cheapest mortise-and-tenon machine available. Mortise-and-tenon joints are used for many types of carcass, such as door frames. Because the table of the drill press (the surface on which the wood rests) can be tilted, holes can also be drilled at an angle.

Two sizes of drill press are available: a floor-standing model (mounted on a column) and a bench model.

Note: Always insist on a demonstration before you purchase the above machinery. Your dealer should also be able to supply a manual providing you with the necessary information for accurate and safe handling of the particular machine .

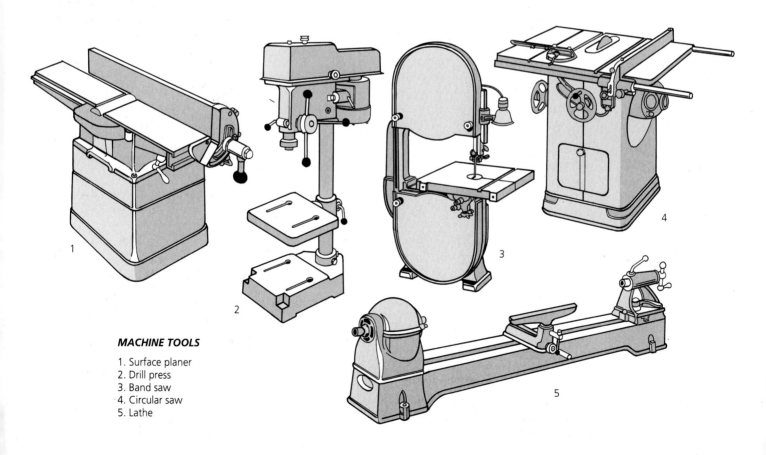

MACHINE TOOLS

1. Surface planer
2. Drill press
3. Band saw
4. Circular saw
5. Lathe

PURCHASING WOOD

PLANED AND UNPLANED WOOD

Most types of wood come in standard dimensions, which differ according to whether the wood has just been sawn (with a rough finish) or planed (also known as PAR: planed all round). Rough or unplaned wood is usually between 3 mm (⅛ in) and 6 mm (¼ in) thicker and wider than planed wood.

There are advantages and disadvantages when purchasing both rough and planed wood. If you purchase rough wood, you will need a surface planer as well as a thicknesser, but the advantage is that you can cut the wood accurately to measure, and even more important, square and true. The advantage of planed wood is that you can see the grain and colour before selecting (unplaned wood is darkened and the grain is not visible). Once a planed board has warped, however, it cannot be planed true without reducing its size, since it has already been cut to a standard thickness. Most timber suppliers will plane your wood at a fixed tariff.

STANDARD DIMENSIONS

The length of wood is given in metres or feet, and the width and thickness in millimetres or inches. Lengths increase in units of 300 mm (1 ft), and widths in units of 30 mm (¼ in). However, the lengths and widths of hardwood are not quite standard. The average available length of oak is ± 2 440 mm (8 ft) and the average available width is 170 mm (6¾ in).

Plywood is available in standard sheets of 2 440 mm x 1 220 mm (8 ft x 4 ft) and in thicknesses of 4 mm (⅛ in), 6 mm (¼ in), 9 mm (⅜ in) and 12 mm (1 in). It can be purchased with a range of veneered finishes, such as oak, from specialist timber merchants. However, it can be very expensive to purchase this way. Chipboard (such as melamine) is available in two sizes: 2 440 mm x 1 220 mm (8 ft x 4 ft) and 2 700 mm x 1 800 mm (8 ft 9 in x 5 ft 10 in). In both cases these are large pieces of wood to handle by yourself, so it is preferable to ask the supplier to cut them to the required size. A special type of saw is needed to saw melamine products to prevent the edges from chipping.

UNITS IN WHICH WOOD IS PURCHASED

Solid wood may be purchased in three different units, namely, per running metre (linear foot), per square metre (square foot) and per cubic metre (cubic foot).

In the case of *cost per running metre (linear foot)*, the cost per cubic metre (cubic foot) would probably already have been determined for boards of a specific thickness and width. To calculate the *costs per square metre (*square foot*)*, the desired width of the board in metres (feet) is multiplied by the length in metres (feet), then multiplied by the price per square metre (square foot).

To calculate the *cost of a board per cubic metre (*cubic foot*)*, the length of the board in metres (feet) is multiplied by width in metres (feet) and then by thickness in metres (feet). This total is then multiplied by the price of the wood per cubic metre (cubic foot). The price of wood board products is always given per square metre (square foot).

HOW TO DRAW UP A SAWING LIST

In each of the projects, the quantity of wood you will require is listed as follows: *quantity x length x width x thickness*.

All boards of the same length, width and thickness are thus grouped together. Let's illustrate this by looking at the wood required for a door. We need two stiles of the same length, width and thickness, which is indicated as follows: 2 x 600 mm x 40 mm x 25 mm (2 ft x 1½ in x 1 in)

The two rails that are required for the door are the same length and thickness, but the width of each differs so they are listed separately: 1 x 400 mm x 40 mm x 25 mm (1 ft 3¾ in x 1½ in x 1 in) *and* 1 x 400 mm x 50 mm x 25 mm (1 ft 3¾ in x 2 in x 1 in)

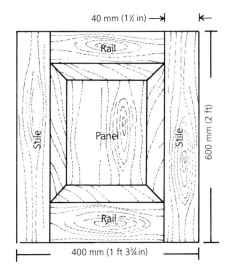

WOODWORK JOINTS

All the joints used for the projects in this book can be divided into five categories:
• Half-lapped (or halving) joints
• Housing (or grooved) joints
• Mortise-and-tenon joints
• Dovetail joints
• Edge joints

HALF-LAPPED JOINTS

Cross-lapped joint This joint is used where rails or shelves cross each other squarely (at 90°).

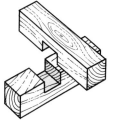 

The joint pulled apart   *The finished joint*

1. Align the two blocks (or boards) and mark-off the thickness on each block in the position where the joint will be. Mark the top half of one block (the bottom piece) and the bottom half of the other block (the top piece) as waste or scrap wood.

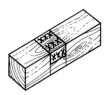 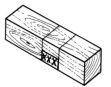

Marked-off blocks

2. Now saw halfway through on the waste wood side of the lines and chisel out the waste wood. First chisel at an angle from both sides and gradually flatten out.

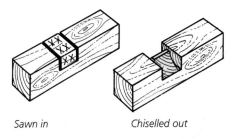

Sawn in   *Chiselled out*

End-lapped joint This is one of the easiest joints which is used in the construction of door frames.

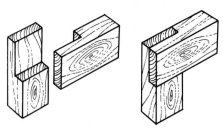

The joint pulled apart   *The finished joint*

1. Mark-off the width of the boards at the end of each board, and then mark-off half the thickness as waste wood.

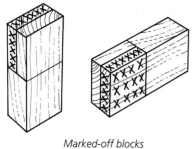

Marked-off blocks

2. Saw out the waste wood with a hand saw or a circular saw.

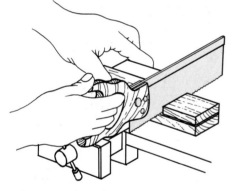

Saw in with the grain

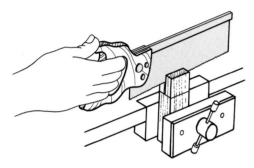

Saw across the grain

HOUSING JOINTS

A stopped housing joint (*see* illustration below) is normally used where shelves are joined to the sides of cabinets, or to the upright sides of a bookshelf.

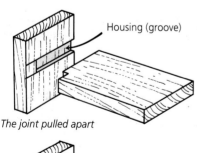

Housing (groove)

The joint pulled apart

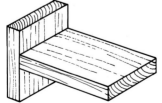

The finished joint

To make the housing

1. Mark-off the position of the housing on the board for the upright by marking-off the thickness of the shelf where it will fit into the housing. Leave a space of approximately 20 mm (¾ in) on the face side of the housing piece of board and mark-off the rest as waste wood. Mark-off the depth of the housing, one-third the thickness of the wood.

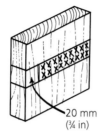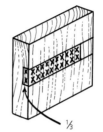

20 mm
(¾ in)

⅓

Marked-off boards

2. To remove the waste wood from the housing, either chisel it out by hand or make use of a router. Place the upright piece of wood flat on the bench, secure it with a G-cramp and chisel out a hole on the waste wood side of the marked lines.

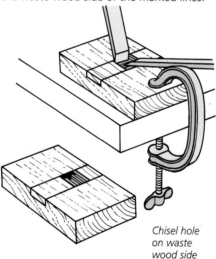

Chisel hole on waste wood side

3. With the upright board still clamped, saw in on the waste wood side of the marked lines, then chisel out the piece between the saw kerfs.

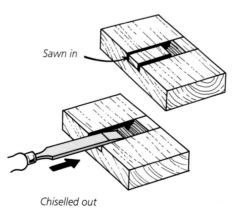

Sawn in

Chiselled out

Sawing the shelf to fit in the housing

4. Now mark-off the depth of the housing (⅓ the thickness of the wood) from the end grain of the shelf, and then mark off about 20 mm (¾ in) from the edge of the shelf to allow for the section between the housing and the edge of the housing piece of board.

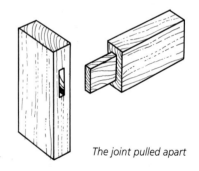

⅓   20 mm (¾ in)

Saw out waste wood at end of shelf

MORTISE-AND-TENON JOINTS

Three kinds of mortise-and-tenon joints are used for the projects in this book: a common mortise-and-tenon joint, a haunched mortise-and-tenon joint and a double mortise-and-tenon joint.

Common mortise-and-tenon joint

This joint consists of a tenon and the mortise into which the tenon fits. The thickness of the tenon must be one-third the thickness of the wood in which it is cut. The depth of the mortise is two-thirds the thickness of the board in which it is cut.

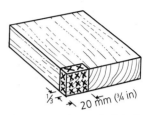

The joint pulled apart

1. Mark-off the tenon by setting the two spurs of a double-point gauge to the same width as a mortise chisel (⅓ of the thickness of the wood). The chisel should fit exactly between the ends of the spurs. Now mark-off the length of the tenon (the same as the depth of the mortise) and draw two lines with the gauge to obtain the thickness of the tenon. Mark-off the length (or position) of the mortise, and, using the same gauge, mark-off the thickness.

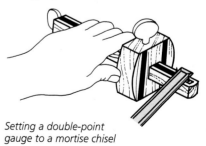

Setting a double-point gauge to a mortise chisel

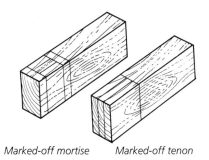

Marked-off mortise   *Marked-off tenon*

2. First cut out the mortise, because if it is skew it can be chiselled square (it will be wider) and the tenon can be adjusted accordingly. Secure the board in a cramp as shown in the illustration below. Begin by chiselling a V-shaped slot in the centre, then cut upright on either side. Use a mortise chisel and a mallet to do this. Repeat the process until the mortise is the correct depth (measure by inserting a steel ruler into the mortise).

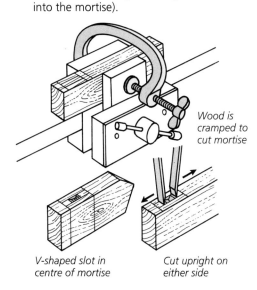

Wood is cramped to cut mortise

V-shaped slot in centre of mortise   *Cut upright on either side*

3. To saw the tenon, place the board at an angle (away from you) in a bench vice. Beginning at the end grain of the board, saw from the middle of the line on the waste wood side, then tilt the saw on your side along the line. The saw will now lie at an angle through the board as illustrated below. Turn the board round and repeat the process. After sawing at an angle from both sides, cramp the block vertically and saw in horizontally. The saw kerfs are illustrated below.

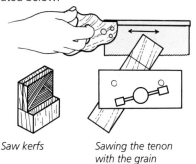

Saw kerfs   *Sawing the tenon with the grain*

4. Now that you have sawn with the grain on either side, saw off the shoulders across the grain.

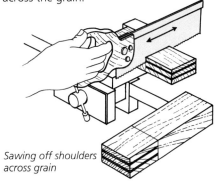

Sawing off shoulders across grain

Haunched mortise-and-tenon joint
This joint is used (without a groove) for tables and (with a groove) for door frames. The mortises are chiselled in the same way as for the common mortise-and-tenon joint and the tenon is also sawn in the same way (*see* above). The illustrations demonstrate how the tenon is marked off, as well as the sequence in which the sawing takes place.

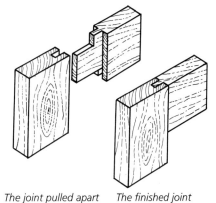

The joint pulled apart   *The finished joint*

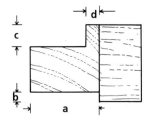

a = ⅔ the width of the wood in which the mortise was cut (length of tenon)
b = 7 mm (⅛ in) (depth of groove)

c = ⅓ the width of the wood after 7 mm (¼ in) has been subtracted
d = 7 mm (¼ in) (or length of the haunch)

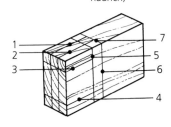

Sequence for sawing in along lines

1. Lines 1 and 2 are drawn together with a double-point gauge. Lines 3 and 4 are drawn separately with a single-point gauge. Lines 5 and 6 (or 7) are drawn around the block with a try square.

The inside groove of the frame can be planed with a plough plane, cut with a router or sawn on a circular saw. The depth of the groove is a standard 7 mm (¼ in) and the width is either equal to the thickness of the tenon, or as wide as the thickness of the panel which fits into it (in a door frame).

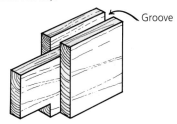

Groove

2. The proportions of the tenon will always determine those of the mortise, since the two fit into each other.

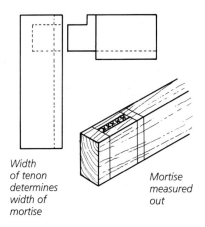

Width of tenon determines width of mortise   *Mortise measured out*

DOVETAIL JOINTS
Two kinds of dovetail joints are used for the projects in this book: the corner dovetail joint and the drawer dovetail joint.

Corner dovetail joint This joint is always made on end grain and is generally used when making a chest or the sides of a drawer (*see* illustration below)

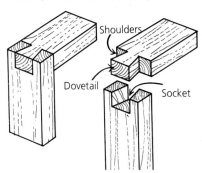

Shoulders
Dovetail
Socket

The finished joint   *The joint pulled apart*

1. First mark-off the dovetail. The length of the tail corresponds with the thickness of the wood in which the socket will be cut, plus a little more – about 1 mm (1⁄16 in). The slope for a dovetail has a ratio of 1:7, that is, for every 7 mm (1⁄4 in) length of tail, 1 mm (1⁄16 in) is measured across and the ends joined to obtain the slope. Mark-off the slope with a sliding bevel. Set the sliding bevel at a slope of 1:7 and push against the end grain of the board to mark-off the slope.

Now turn over the sliding bevel and mark-off the slope on the other side. To saw out the dovetail, place the board in a bench vice with the waste wood on the right-hand side and saw in with the grain. Then saw the shoulders across the grain.

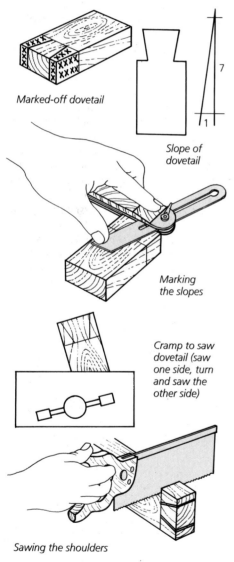

Marked-off dovetail

Slope of dovetail

Marking the slopes

Cramp to saw dovetail (saw one side, turn and saw the other side)

Sawing the shoulders

2. Once you have sawn the dovetail, mark it off clearly on the end grain of the other board to indicate the lines for the socket. The depth of the socket must always correspond with the thickness of the dovetail board, plus 1 mm (1⁄16 in).

3. To make the socket, first saw in with the grain and then chisel out the waste wood in between.

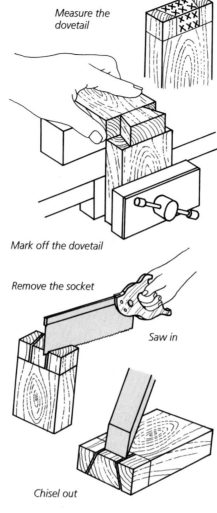

Measure the dovetail

Mark off the dovetail

Remove the socket

Saw in

Chisel out

Drawer dovetail

This joint is made in the face of a drawer and for the carcass of a cabinet.

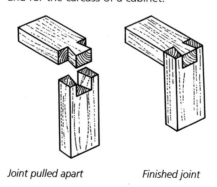

Joint pulled apart   *Finished joint*

1. The slope of the tail is the same as that of a corner dovetail joint (1:7) but the dovetail is shorter (two-thirds of the thickness of the wood in which the socket will be cut). Saw out the dovetail and mark it the same way as the corner dovetail (*see above*). Only the socket is different, as it is sawn in diagonally and then chiselled out.

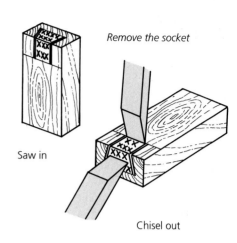

Remove the socket

Saw in

Chisel out

EDGE JOINTS

Most solid wood boards are not wide enough to make articles with a large surface area (for example, a table top), and therefore have to be glued-up edge-to-edge laterally.

1. The mating edges of this joint are planed square and true (at 90°) and glued together laterally. This joint is also called a *butt joint* and can be reinforced by grooving both edges (after planing) and glueing a loose piece or tongue of wood or plywood between the boards.

2. Check whether the joint fits, then glue and secure the wood in a cramp or vice.

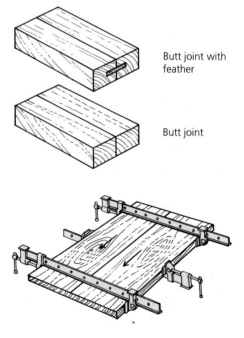

Butt joint with feather

Butt joint

Glued up and cramped boards

Note: Making edge joints can be a difficult task if you do not have the right machine tools. If this is the case, have the joint done at a joinery or carpenter's workshop.

MISCELLANEOUS CONSTRUCTION METHODS

Other methods include those additional constructions associated with the carcass, such as for drawers, doors, panels and mouldings.

DRAWER CONSTRUCTION

A drawer consists of a face (front), a back, sides and a bottom. These form a box which must fit and slide into an opening in a table, chest or cabinet. Therefore, it must correspond with this opening (on completion of the table, chest or cabinet). Here are two construction methods: one simple and the other more complex.

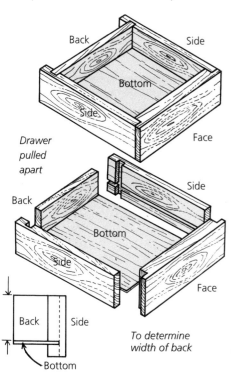

Drawer pulled apart

To determine width of back

Simple construction method

1. First cut the face to fit into the cabinet opening. It must be an exact fit, since it is visible on the outside. Then make the sides so that they slide in comfortably. Plane the grooves in the sides and face (for the bottom to fit into). The height of the back must extend from above the groove to the top of the side. Its length is the same as that of the face. The thickness of the sides and the back (measuring 14-16 mm or about ½ in) are less than that of the face, which is 20 mm (¾ in).

2. Place the end grain of the back against the sides and mark-off the thickness. Cut a housing between the lines to a depth that is half the thickness of the side by sawing between the lines and then chiselling out the waste wood horizontally. Repeat this procedure with the other side.

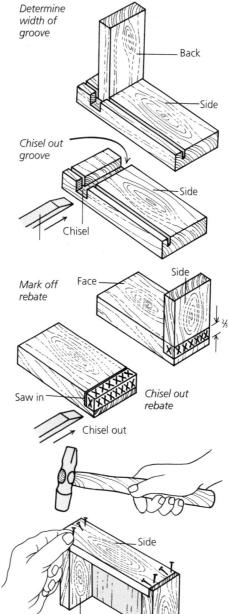

Determine width of groove

Chisel out groove

Mark off rebate

Chisel out rebate

Assembly of construction

3. House the ends of the sides in the face by making a corner rebate. The rebate must extend to two-thirds the thickness of the face, while its depth must correspond with the thickness of the side. Mark-off the end of the side on the end of the face. Set a marking gauge at two-thirds the thickness of the face and mark-off on the end of the face.

4. Make the rebate by sawing in on the waste wood side (two-thirds deep) and then chiselling it out from the side. The drawer is now ready for assembling. It is held together with panel pins and glue. Drive the pins in at an angle so that the

parts do not pull away easily from each other. Make sure that the sides and the face are true (at 90° with each other).

5. Once you have assembled the carcass of the drawer (the face, sides and back) and the glue has dried, mark the shape off on plywood to determine the dimensions of the bottom. Mark-off the inside of the carcass and add the depth of the grooves and the thickness of the back, then cut the plywood along the markings.

6. Slide the bottom under the back and into the sides and face. Fasten the bottom to the back with screws (so that it can be removed if necessary).

Complex construction method

1. A more complicated carcass involves using dovetail joints instead of rebates or corner rebates. Most important here is marking-off the sides of the drawer, which house the dovetails and grooves.

The dovetails at the face are part of a drawer dovetail joint (*see page 14*). To mark-off more than one dovetail, choose the shoulder width and mark-off the length of the dovetails. Draw a diagonal line from the shoulder width to the opposite side of the drawer side. The length of this line must be a multiple of the number of dovetails. Divide this line in half for two dovetails, and draw a line parallel with the edge of the board towards the shoulder line. Mark-off the shoulder from the opposite side of the board, and from the dividing line. Mark-off the slopes obtained from these points (*see illustration below*).

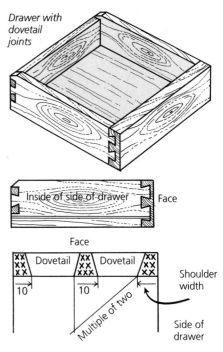

Drawer with dovetail joints

Mark off two dovetail joints

2. Now mark-off the width of the groove with a double-point gauge. The bottom of the groove runs through the narrow side of the bottom dovetail (*see* illustration below).

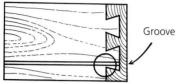

Side of drawer

Groove

To determine height of groove

3. All you need now is for the corner dovetail to fit into the back of the drawer. Mark-off the end of the back on to the back of the side of the drawer. The back must stretch from above the groove to just below the top edge (to allow for the circulation of air when the drawer is closed). Once you have marked this position, mark-off the shoulder width from the top and the bottom to obtain the width of the dovetail, and mark-off the slopes.

Back of drawer

Back

Side of drawer

To determine position of back

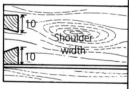

10

Shoulder width

10

Mark-off dovetail joint

4. The side of the drawer has been marked-off. Saw and chisel the dovetails and plane the grooves. Now mark-off the dovetails on the top edges of the face and back (*see* Dovetail joints, page 13), and saw and chisel the sockets. Assemble the carcass of the drawer and insert the bottom as described in the simpler construction method (see page 15).

Securing the drawer in a cramp
5. It is not necessary to cramp the carcass that was made using the simpler method, since it is fastened with panel pins. However, the more complicated carcass must be secured in a cramp from the end of the dovetails at the face to the end of the dovetails at the back (*see* illustration). Secure both sides of the drawer in the cramp at the same time.

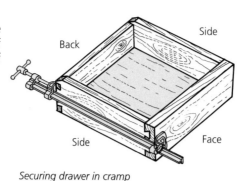

Back

Side

Side

Face

Securing drawer in cramp

DOOR CONSTRUCTION (FOR A CABINET)
As for drawer construction, two construction methods are explained – one which is simple and the other more complicated.

Simple construction method
The simple carcass (as shown in the illustration below) is made using end-lapped joints (*see* page 11).

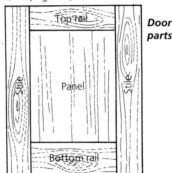

Top rail

Door parts

Stile

Panel

Stile

Bottom rail

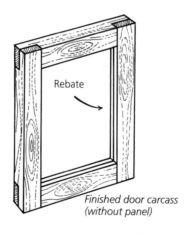

Rebate

Finished door carcass (without panel)

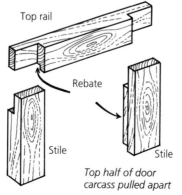

Top rail

Rebate

Stile

Stile

Top half of door carcass pulled apart

1. First plane a rebate (use a rebate plane, or a router) in all four parts (rails and stiles) of the door. Mark-off all the ends of the stiles (that is, the full width of the stile) on to the ends of the rails and mark-off the ends of the rails (width minus depth of rebate) on to the ends of the stiles.

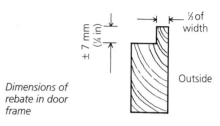

± 7 mm (¼ in)

⅓ of width

Outside

Dimensions of rebate in door frame

2. Mark-off half the width at all the ends. Now saw out the back half of the stiles and the front half of the railings. The small hole that inevitably occurs at the top can be filled in later (*see* illustration below).

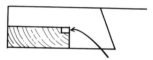

Small hole at top of door

3. Secure the frame at all four corners with G-cramps. Make sure the door is resting on a level surface. First assemble the joints to check that everything fits, then glue and secure. The panel can be fitted later, as it is housed in a rebate. It is fastened with a small strip of wood, as illustrated below.

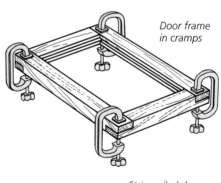

Door frame in cramps

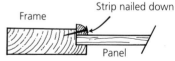

Frame

Strip nailed down

Panel

Securing panel

Complex construction method
1. With this method, haunched mortise-and-tenon joints are used (*see* page 13). First plane the stiles to measure, and then saw them to length (of the cabinet opening), but retain a small piece of waste wood (a horn) at each top edge after the length has been marked off. Place the stiles together and measure the mortises.

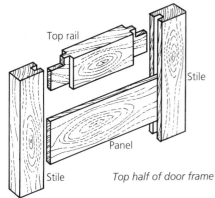

Top rail

Stile

Panel

Stile

Top half of door frame

2. First cut all four mortises (*see* Mortise-and-tenon joints, page 12), then plane the railings to width and mark the length of the rails. The length of the rails can be marked off on the stiles in the cabinet (*see* illustration below).

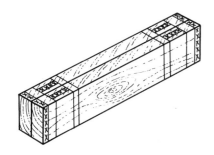

Stiles placed together to mark off mortises

3. Mark-off the shoulder width (distance between stiles) and add the lengths of the tenons on both sides. Now mark-off the tenons and saw them (*see* pages 12-13). Plane the grooves with a plough plane. The door is now ready for assembling in a cramp (do not glue yet) to check whether it is square and true. Mark-off the inside of the door on the wood and add the depth of the mortise all round to determine the dimensions of the panel. Because the panel fits into a groove, this frame is glued up round the panel, and the panel should always be planed before the door is glued. Secure the door frame in a cramp from the ends of the tenons to the opposite ends of the tenons.

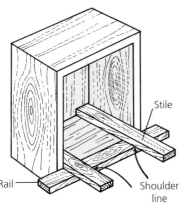

Stile

Rail

Shoulder line

To determine length of rails

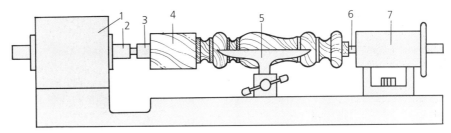

Parts of a lathe
1. Headstock
2. Headstock spindle
3. Driving centre
4. Turning piece
5. Tool rest
6. Tailstock centre
7. Tailstock

TURNING WOOD

TURNING A TABLE LEG

1. Plane the wood as square as possible.

2. Find the centre of the square piece of wood by drawing diagonal lines (see illustration below).

Draw diagonal lines

3. Use a full-scale sketch of the leg on a piece of cardboard to mark-off the length on to the wood (*see* illustration).

4. Mount the wood between the centres on the lathe.

5. Begin by rounding off the part of the wood that will finally be the shaped section of the leg.

6. Mark-off the lengths from the sketch on to the wood (*see* illustration).

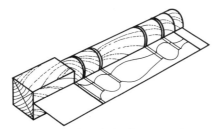

Leg sketched and marked off onto wood

7. Cut the wood to the correct diameter with a paring tool. To find the diameter, set a pair of outside callipers to the diameter on the sketch and check for accuracy on the wood (*see* illustration).

Setting outside callipers to sketch

Checking diameter of coves with outside calipers

8. Now turn the rest of the shape (*see* Woodturning tools and their functions, below). Sand the leg and polish it, if necessary, on the lathe.

WOODTURNING TOOLS AND THEIR FUNCTIONS

A **gouging tool** is used to turn a square piece of wood into a round shape and hollow out concave shapes.

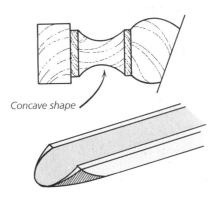

Concave shape

Gouging tool

A **paring tool** is used to make coves and to scribe lines on wood.

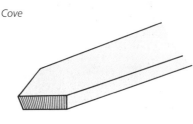

Cove

Paring tool

A **round-nosed scraper** is used to turn concave shapes and to turn shoulders away for convex shapes.

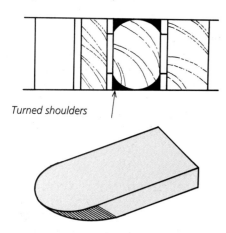

Turned shoulders

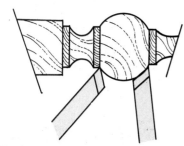

Round-nosed scraper

The function of a **skew chisel** is to turn convex shapes.

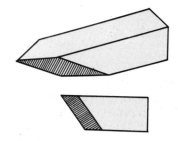

Turning convex shapes

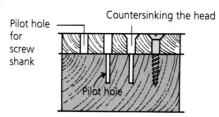

Skew chisel

OTHER MATERIALS

NAILS

Nails are used in most phases of a project to keep parts of a construction in position until the glue has dried. Usually panel pins are used for this purpose because they are thin and do not crack the wood. The heads are small and can easily be sunk below the surface with the aid of a nail punch. Afterwards, the hole can be filled with a wood filler.

In most cases, nails are dovetailed or skewed, which means that the nails are knocked in at an angle to prevent the board from coming loose (*see* illustration).

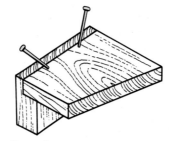

Dovetailing nails

SCREWS

Countersunk screws – where the head of the screw is countersunk until it is flush with or just below the surface of the wood – are normally used for fastening wood.

When securing two boards with screws, drive the screw loosely through the first board, and then screw it into the second one. It will be easier to do this if you drill a small hole (pilot hole) into the second board and grease the end of the screw. Ream (enlarge) the hole with a countersink so that the head of the screw fits exactly (*see* illustration).

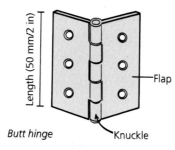

Screwing in

HINGES

Generally, ordinary brass butt hinges are used. The size of the hinge is determined by the size of the door. Available sizes (in length) are 50 mm (2 in), 75 mm (3 in) and 100 mm (4 in).

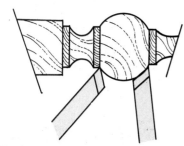

Length (50 mm/2 in)

Flap

Butt hinge

Knuckle

To attach a hinge to a door, either house the flaps equally into the door and the door frame, or house only the total thickness of the knuckle into the door.

1. Mark the position of the hinge on the door (*see* illustration). Using a marking gauge, mark-off the thickness of the knuckle (a) in the width of the flap up to the middle of the knuckle (b) just above the bottom rail and just below the top rail.

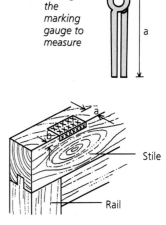

Setting the marking gauge to measure

b

a

Stile

Rail

Marking the position of a hinge on a door

2. Now saw in and chisel out the recess for the hinge.

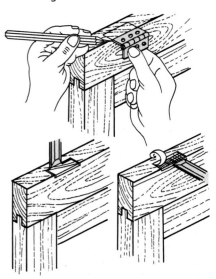

Sawing in recess   *Chiselling out recess*

3. Before screwing the hinge into the door, remember to drill pilot holes first. Now place the door with the hinge attached into the cabinet opening and mark the position of the hinge where it is going to be fastened to the cabinet (*see* illustration above for clarification).

Set a marking gauge to measure (a) and mark-off on the cabinet. Hold the flap of the hinge inside the frame and mark the position of the pilot holes. As before, drill pilot holes and screw the hinge into position by opening the door and resting the hinge in the small frame (*see* illustration).

Always make sure that the heads of the screws are not too large for the hinge, otherwise they cannot be countersunk properly. Insert one screw into each hinge flap and, in order to make sure that the fit is correct, close the door. If it fits flush, you may go ahead and countersink the remaining screws.

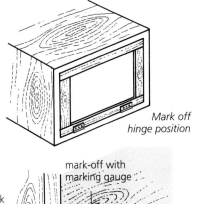

Mark off hinge position

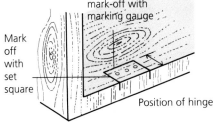

Mark off with set square

mark-off with marking gauge

Position of hinge

Mark off where flap of hinge fits in cabinet and position of holes

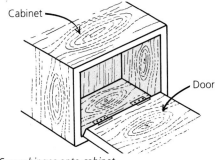

Cabinet

Door

Screw hinges onto cabinet

CATCHES AND HANDLES

If you decide to turn your own *doorknobs* on a lathe, turn them with a dowel that will fit into the slot of a predetermined size that has been drilled into the stiles of the door. Glue the dowel into the slot.

Ready-made knobs and *handles* have a machined screw that turns into a recess in the knob. Turn the screw from the inside of the door through a slot in the knob (*see* illustration).

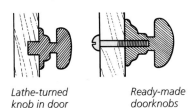

Lathe-turned knob in door

Ready-made doorknobs

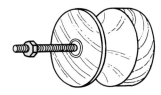

Fastening ready-made knobs

Position the knob on a door two-thirds from the top of the door, if the door is to hang above head height, and two-thirds from the bottom, if the door is to hang below head height (*see* illustration).

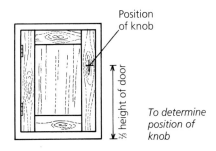

Position of knob

⅔ height of door

To determine position of knob

Catches are required to keep a door shut. However, they are generally used for doors without locks.

Different kinds of catches are illustrated below. They should preferably be fastened in an unobtrusive place, for example, under a shelf. Fasten one part to the cabinet and the other part (the plate) to the door. Make sure the two parts are exactly opposite each other.

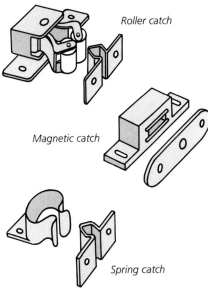

Roller catch

Magnetic catch

Spring catch

FINISHING AND POLISHING

FINISHING

Finishing involves removing all visible machine marks with a plane or scraper, and sanding the article. Sand all the components before glueing, then smooth the joints and give the article a final sanding. Filling small holes where the heads of panel pins have been countersunk, also forms part of the finishing process (*see* Belt sander, page 9 for hint on filling these holes).

An article should be sanded with different grades (grits) of sandpaper, ranging from rough (60 grits) to fine (150 grits). Sand with a belt sander to remove rough

marks and then with an orbital sander, using fine sandpaper. It is best to do the final finishing by hand. Mouldings can often only be sanded by hand.

POLISHING

Once an article has been neatly finished, cover it with a protective finishing layer to prevent marking or staining, to seal the wood and to enhance its appearance.

If you polish an article by hand, there are two kinds of finishes you can use: oil or polyurethane varnish.

Oil polish

There are many ready-made furniture oils available which can be applied with a brush or a buffing pad (*see* illustration). The more coats applied, the better the finish. A certain number of these oils contain dissolved wax that leaves a protective waterproof layer on the wood.

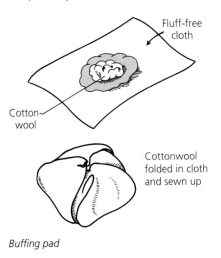

Fluff-free cloth

Cotton-wool

Cottonwool folded in cloth and sewn up

Buffing pad

Polyurethane varnish

For the first layer, thin the varnish with about 50% turpentine and apply with a brush or a buffing pad. When it is dry, smooth with steel wool or fine sandpaper and apply a second layer of pure varnish.

Apply another two layers as described above for a glossy effect. Finish off by applying white floor polish to give the article a protective wax layer.

For furniture, the best finish is obtained by spraying. A lacquered varnish containing a catalyst is normally used. This finish dries very quickly but, unfortunately, cannot be applied by hand.

Staining wood

Sanded furniture may be stained to match other items. Your hardware supplier will help you choose from the various types of colouring agents available. Stain is applied evenly with a cloth or brush and the excess is wiped away. When properly dry, the article may be oiled or varnished.

KEY RACK

A key rack is probably one of the easiest woodwork projects imaginable, and it is a most useful object to have in the home. Keys are forever being mislaid and more often than not they disappear for good. Place the rack close to the front door and get into the habit of hanging your keys there when you enter the house.

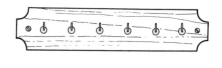

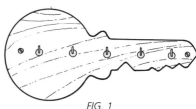

FIG. 1
Alternative designs

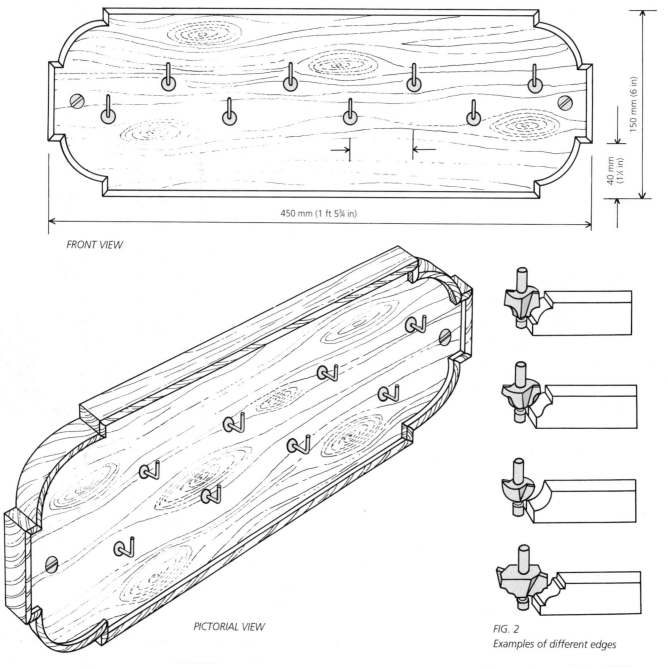

150 mm (6 in)

40 mm (1½ in)

450 mm (1 ft 5¾ in)

FRONT VIEW

PICTORIAL VIEW

FIG. 2
Examples of different edges

Use any wood of your choice.

Materials
1 x 450 mm x 150 mm x 20 mm
 (1 ft 5¾ in x 6 in x ¾ in) piece wood
Sandpaper and varnish
8 hooks
2 wall plugs
2 screws (to screw into the wall)

Construction
1. Cut the wood to measure.

2. Sketch the chosen shape on paper (see figure 1).

3. Trace the shape on to the wood.

4. Saw out the shape with a jig saw.

5. Finish the edge and shape with a router (see figure 2).

6. Mark the position of the hooks and drill pilot holes.

7. Mark and drill the holes for the screws to attach the key rack to the wall.

8. Sand the rack with fine sandpaper.

9. Varnish the rack (see Polishing on page 19).

10. Turn in the hooks.

11. Fix the key rack to the wall with plugs and screws.

HALL STAND

This hall stand not only provides a place to hang coats and hats, but also includes a framed mirror, a table top and a drawer. You can adjust this design to match different furniture styles.

Oak was the principal timber used for this project; pine was used for the drawers.

Materials

2 x 1 900 mm x 80 mm x 20 mm
(6 ft 3 in x 3¼ in x ¾ in) pieces oak
for parts A and B

2 x 810 mm x 70 mm x 20 mm
(2 ft 8 in x 2¾ in x ¾ in) pieces oak
for parts D and F

1 x 810 mm x 100 mm x 20 mm
(2 ft 8 in x 4 in x ¾ in) piece oak
for part C

1 x 810 mm x 190 mm x 20 mm (2 ft 8
in x 7½ in x ¾ in) piece oak for part E

2 x 680 mm x 70 mm x 20 mm
(2 ft 3 in x 2¾ in x ¾ in) pieces oak
for parts G and H

4 x 420 mm x 70 mm x 20 mm
(1 ft 4½ in x 2¾ in x ¾ in) pieces oak
for parts I, J, K and L

2 x 840 mm x 70 mm x 20 mm
(2 ft 9 in x 2¾ in x ¾) pieces oak for
parts M and N

2 x 800 mm x 50 mm x 50 mm
(2 ft 7½ in x 2 in x 2 in) pieces oak
for front legs

2 x 130 mm x 400 mm x 20 mm
(5 in x 1 ft 3¾ in x ¾ in) pieces oak
for parts O and P

4 x 330 mm x 60 mm x 20 mm
(1 ft 1 in x 2¼ in x ¾ in) pieces oak
for parts Q, R, S and T

4 x 280 mm x 20 mm x 20 mm
(11 in x ¾ in x ¾ in) pieces oak for
parts U, V, W and X

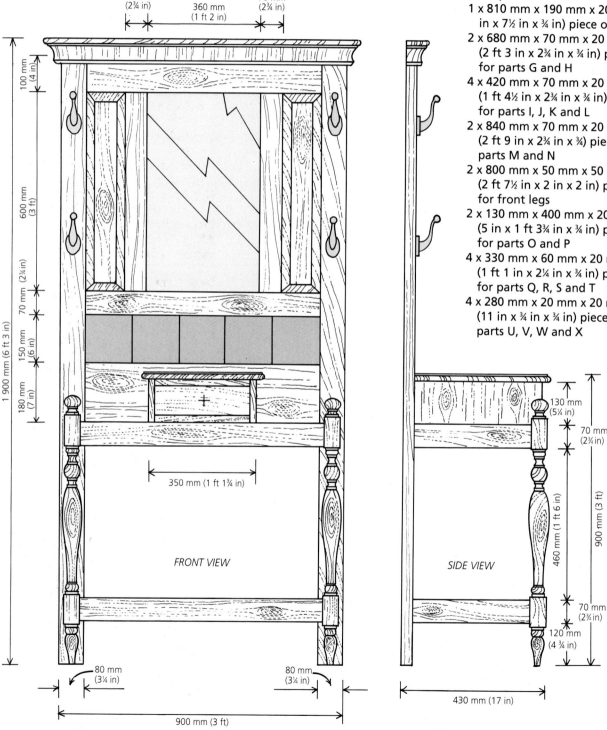

FRONT VIEW

SIDE VIEW

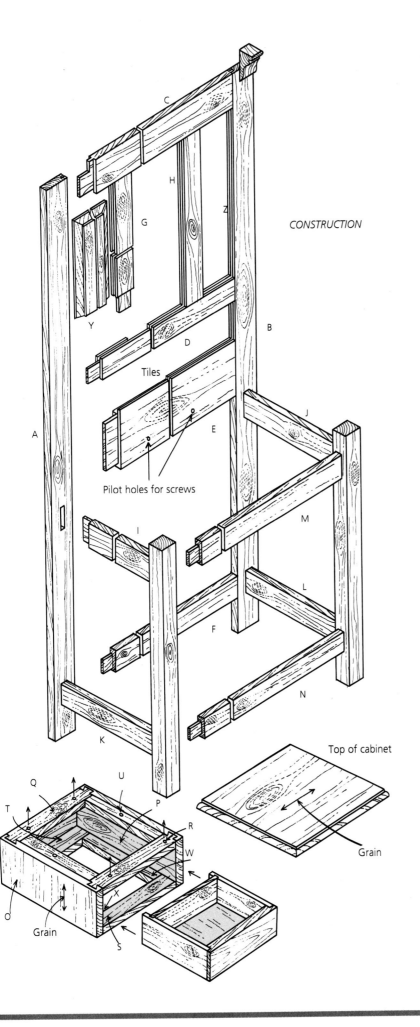

CONSTRUCTION

Tiles

Pilot holes for screws

Top of cabinet

Grain

Grain

1 x 400 mm x 43 mm x 20 mm
  (1 ft 3¾ in x 1¾ in x ¾ in) pieces oak
  for tabletop
1 x 950 mm x 80 mm x 32 mm
  (3 ft 1½ in x 3¼ in x 1¼ in) piece oak
  for moulding at top of back frame
  (or ready-made crown moulding)
2 x 625 mm x 140 mm x 16 mm
  (2 ft ¾ in x 5½ in x ½ in) pieces oak
  for parts Y and Z
1 x 300 mm x 90 mm x 20 mm
  (12 in x 3½ in x ¾ in) piece oak for
  front of drawer
2 x 350 mm x 90 mm x 15 mm
  (1 ft 1¾ in x 3½ in x ½ in) pieces pine
  for sides of drawer
1 x 300 mm x 70 mm x 15 mm
  (12 in x 2¾ in x ½ in) piece pine for
  back of drawer
1 x 350 mm x 300 mm x 7 mm
  (1 ft 1¾ in x 12 in x ¼ in) piece
  plywood for bottom of drawer
5 x 150 mm x 150 mm (6 in x 6 in)
  ceramic tiles of your choice
1 x mirror
  (610 mm x 370 mm/23¾ in x 14¼ in)
Sandpaper
10 (30 mm/1¼ in x no. 8) countersunk
  screws to fix top and cabinet part
Woodworking adhesive
4 brass hooks (see figure 6)
Varnish or furniture oil

Back frame

1. Mark off the tenons and mortises for
the back frame: for rails C, D, E, F, G and
H and stiles A and B (see Mortise-and-
tenon joints, page 12). At the tenons of
rails C, D, E, G and H, make provision for
mortises by leaving shoulders of at least
7 mm (¼ in) (see figure 1).

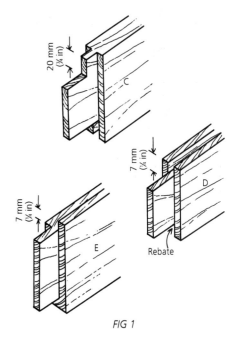

FIG 1

2. Make the mortises and tenons for the back frame.

3. Plane the grooves for the panels and tiles, using a plough plane.

4. Plane the rebate for the mirror with a rebate plane or router.

5. Cut the boards for the panels (Y and Z) to measure and plane to thickness.

6. Plane the panels. Determine the width of the raised part and saw in until about 4 mm (⅛ in) deep. Plane the edges to thickness, using a rebate plane (see figure 2).

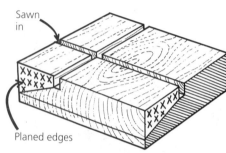

Marked off

Sawn in

Planed edges

Fits in groove

Corner of panel when finished

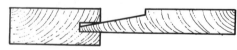

Panel in frame
FIG. 2

7. The parts of the frame can now be glued and cramped. Remember, the frame is glued around the panels. The tiles are fixed into the frame with a wooden strip (list) at a later stage (see step 25).

Table section
8. Trace the shape of the front legs and turn on a lathe (see Turning a table leg, page 17).

9. Mark off the tenons and mortises for rails I, J, K, L, M and N.

10. Chisel the mortises and saw the tenons (see Mortise-and-tenon joints, page 12).

11. Sand the table parts.

12. Cramp and glue the table parts together, and then to the back frame.

Cabinet section
13. Now glue together parts O and P (the sides) and saw them to measure (see Edge joints, page 14).

14. Saw and plane rails Q, R, S and T to measure and mark-off the dovetails.

15. Saw out the dovetails and trace them on to the sides. Saw and chisel the sockets.

16. Saw and plane parts U, V, W and X to measure so that they fit between the rails.

17. Sand all the parts for the cabinet, cramp and glue together.

18. Glue the top of the cabinet, and saw to measure (see Edge joints, page 14).

19. Sand the top and screw it to the cabinet through the rails.

20. Shape the edge of the top with a router (see figure 3).

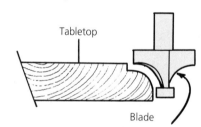

Tabletop

Blade

FIG. 3

21. Screw the cabinet to rail E of the back frame and glue on to rail M (see figure 4).

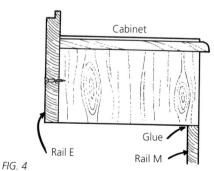

Cabinet

Glue

Rail E   *Rail M*

FIG. 4

Drawer
22. Plane the parts of the drawer to measure, mark-off the joints and construct the drawer. Consult Drawer construction on page 15 for clarification if necessary.

23. Glue and cramp the drawer and slide the bottom in.

24. Fix a knob or handle to the drawer.

Tiles and mirror
25. Fix the tiles into the frame with a wooden strip (see figure 5).

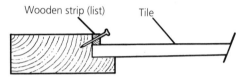

Wooden strip (list)   *Tile*

FIG. 5

26. Fix the mirror into the frame

Hooks
26. Screw brass hooks (see figure 6) into the back frame.

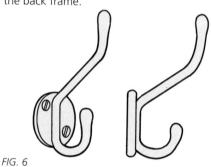

FIG. 6

Crown moulding
27. A crown moulding requires sophisticated machining, so you can either buy a ready-made one or use the piece of oak to make one yourself. Glue it on to the back frame and join at an angle of 45° at the corners (see figure 7).

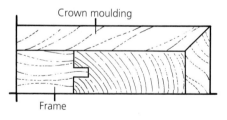

Crown moulding

Frame

FIG. 7

Finishing and polishing
28. Now give all the parts of the assembled hall stand a final sanding with fine sandpaper (120 grits).

29. Varnish or oil the hall stand (see Polishing, page 19).

HALL TABLE WITH DRAWERS

This multi-purpose hall table could stand in an entrance hall or in a wide passage. It can be used as a telephone table, and, if you hang a framed mirror on the wall above it, it could even serve as a dressing table. Modify the design by choosing a different shape for the legs and by using a lighter-coloured wood.

Any suitable hardwood and pine can be used for this project.

Materials
4 x 750 mm x 60 mm x 60 mm
  (2 ft 5½ in x 2¼ in x 2¼ in) pieces
  hardwood for legs
1 x 820 mm x 130 mm x 20 mm
  (2 ft 8¼ in x 5¼ in x ¾ in) piece
  hardwood for back rail
2 x 440 mm x 130 mm x 20 mm
  (1 ft 5½ in x 5¼ in x ¾ in) pieces
  hardwood for side rails
2 x 820 mm x 80 mm x 20 mm
  (2 ft 8¼ in x 3¼ in x ¾ in) pieces
  hardwood for top and bottom
  rails of drawer
1 x 414 mm x 130 mm x 20 mm
  (1 ft 4 in x 5¼ in x ¾ in) piece pine
  for horizontal divider

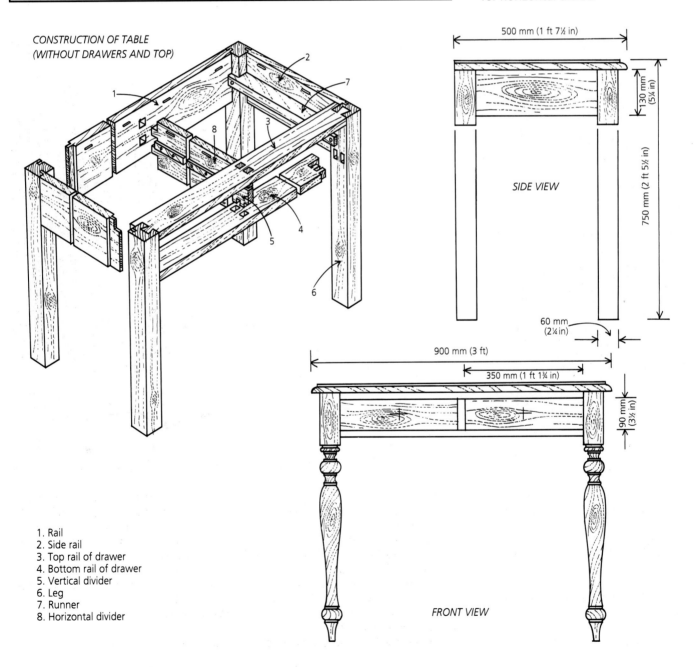

CONSTRUCTION OF TABLE
(WITHOUT DRAWERS AND TOP)

500 mm (1 ft 7½ in)

130 mm (5¼ in)

SIDE VIEW

750 mm (2 ft 5½ in)

60 mm (2¼ in)

900 mm (3 ft)

350 mm (1 ft 1¾ in)

90 mm (3½ in)

FRONT VIEW

1. Rail
2. Side rail
3. Top rail of drawer
4. Bottom rail of drawer
5. Vertical divider
6. Leg
7. Runner
8. Horizontal divider

1 x 130 mm x 80 mm x 20 mm
(5¼ in x 3¼ in x ¾ in) piece hardwood
for vertical divider

2 x 440 mm x 45 mm x 19 mm
(1 ft 5½ in x 1¾ in x ¾ in) pieces pine
for runners

2 x 440 x 5 mm x 19 mm (1 ft 5½ in
x ¼ in x ¾ in) pieces pine for runners

1 x 900 mm x 500 mm x 20 mm
(3 ft x 1 ft 7½ in x ¾ in) piece
hardwood for tabletop

2 x 360 mm x 90 mm x 20 mm
(1 ft 2 in x 3½ in x ¾ in) pieces
hardwood for drawer faces

4 x 440 mm x 90 mm x 15 mm
(1 ft 5½ in x 3½ in x ½ in) pieces pine
for sides of drawers

2 x 360 mm x 70 mm x 15 mm
(1 ft 2 in x 2¾ in x ½ in) pieces pine
for back of drawers

2 x 425 mm x 345 mm x 7 mm
(1 ft 4¾ in x 1 ft 1¾ in x ¼ in) pieces

pine plywood for bottom of drawers

14 fasteners (to secure table top)

14 (20 mm/¾ in x no. 8) countersunk
screws (to secure fasteners)

2 knobs or 4 handles (for drawers)

Panel pins (40 mm/1½ in) if you are
using the simple drawer construction
method

Woodworking adhesive

Sandpaper

Varnish or furniture oil

Legs

1. Shape the legs. If you are going to turn the legs on a lathe, first make a sketch (*see* Turning a table leg, page 17 and Dining-room table, pages 44-6) before turning.

2. Mark off the mortises on the legs where the tenons for the side and back rails will fit (*see* Mortise-and-tenon joints, page 12 and Dining-room table, pages 44-46).

3. Chisel out the mortises or drill with a mortising machine (*see* Drill press, page 10), and saw out the groove for the haunched parts of the tenon (*see* Haunched mortise-and-tenon joint, page 13).

Rails

4. Mark-off the tenons for the side and back rails (*see* Haunched mortise-and-tenon joint, page 13).

5. Saw the tenons (*see* Mortise-and-tenon joint, page 12).

6. Mark-off the dovetails for the drawer's top rail, then saw and chisel out.

7. Mark-off the double tenon for the bottom drawer rail (*see* figure 1). Mark-off the dimensions of the leg on the end. Deduct two x the width of the tenons (10 mm/⅜ in) from the leg width – 60 mm (2¼ in) – and divide the remainder by three to determine the shoulder widths. Saw out the tenons.

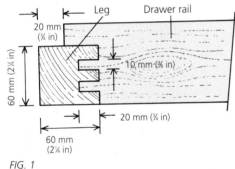

FIG. 1

Removing dovetail sockets and the mortises for double tenons

8. Mark-off the dovetail joints for the top rail on the end grain of the front legs (*see* figure 2).

9. Saw and chisel out the tenons.

10. Mark-off the double tenons of the bottom drawer rails to determine the position of the mortises (*see* figure 3).

11. Chisel out the mortises for the double tenons.

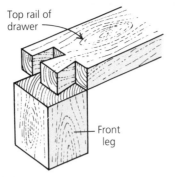

FIG. 2

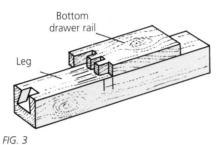

FIG. 3

Dividers

12. Mark-off the mortises and tenons for the vertical divider in the same way as for the bottom drawer rail (*see* step 10). Saw the tenons and chisel out the mortises.

13. Now mark-off the double tenons at the back of the horizontal divider (*see* example in figure 4).

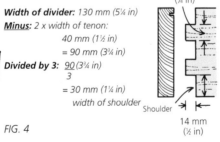

Width of divider: 130 mm (5¼ in)
Minus: 2 x width of tenon:
40 mm (1½ in)
= 90 mm (3¾ in)
Divided by 3: $\frac{90}{3}$ (3¾ in)
= 30 mm (1¼ in)
width of shoulder

FIG. 4

14. Saw the double tenons and mark-off to determine the position of the mortises (*see* step 10).

15. Chisel out the mortises in the back rail.

16. The front end of the horizontal divider must fit into the vertical divider with a mortise-and-tenon joint (*see* figure 5). Saw the tenon and chisel out the mortise in the vertical divider.

Carcass

17. Chisel out the slots for the fasteners. The table carcass is now ready to be sanded, glued and cramped. First cramp the back rail between the back legs, and the top and bottom drawer rails (with the divider) between the front legs. When the

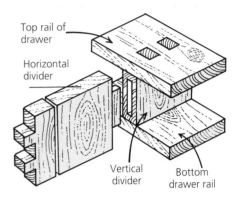

FIG. 5

glue has dried, cramp and glue the side rails and the horizontal divider across the front and back legs.

18. Now saw and screw the drawer runners to measure (to match the carcass). Check with a small spirit level to make sure they are all horizontal.

Table top

19. Glue, saw to measure, plane and sand the table top (*see* Edge joints, page 14).

20. Secure the top to the carcass with fasteners (*see* Dining-room table, page 44-46). Shape the edge of the top with a router.

Drawers

21. Mark-off the parts of the drawers to correspond with the openings in the table carcass. Mark-off and make the joints, and assemble the carcass of the drawers (*see* Drawer construction, page 15). Fix the knobs or handles to the drawer faces (*see* Catches and handles, page 19). Make housing joints in the sides of the drawers (as wide as the width of the runner) so that they can slide on the runners (*see* figure 6). Use either a plough plane or a router to make this housing.

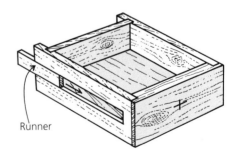

FIG. 6

Finishing and polishing

22. Sand the table with fine sandpaper and polish with varnish or oil (*see* Polishing, page 19).

TELEPHONE TABLE

This versatile table not only provides a special place for a telephone, but has a cabinet to keep directories and writing materials at hand. The convenient built-in seat means that you don't have to fetch a chair before you can sit down and enjoy your conversation. For comfort, make a cushion by cutting a piece of foam to measure and covering it in fabric of your choice.

Oak, pine, and chipboard were used for this project.

Materials

2 x 900 mm x 60 mm x 25 mm
(3 ft x 2¼ in x 1 in) pieces oak for length rails of seat frame

3 x 450 mm x 60 mm x 25 mm
(1 ft 5¾ in x 2¼ in x 1 in) pieces oak for cross-rails of seat frame

4 x 430 mm x 60 mm x 25 mm
(1 ft 5¾ in x 2¼ in x 1 in) pieces oak for uprights for legs

2 x 425 mm x 60 mm x 25 mm
(1 ft 4¾ in x 2¼ in x 1 in) pieces oak for horizontals for legs

4 x 412 mm x 20 mm x 20 mm
(1 ft 4 in x ¾ in x ¾ in) pieces oak for mouldings on inside of frame (or ready-made equivalent)

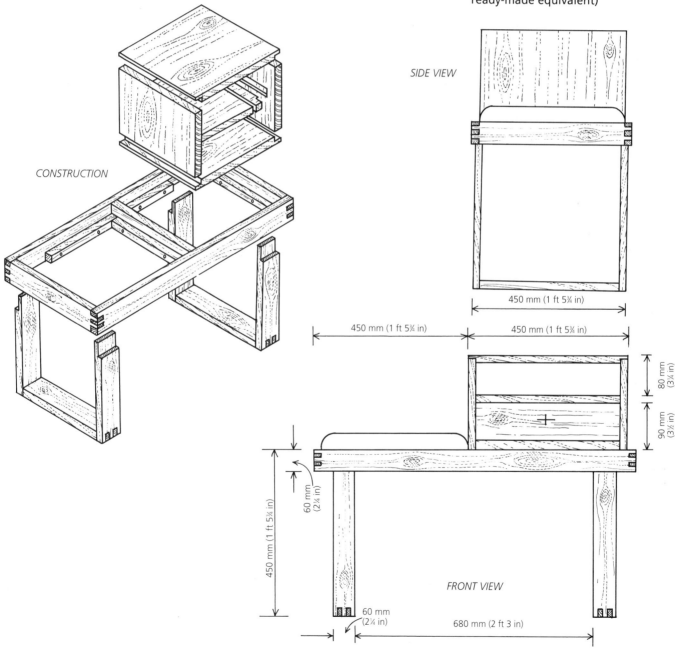

CONSTRUCTION

SIDE VIEW

450 mm (1 ft 5¾ in)

450 mm (1 ft 5¾ in)

450 mm (1 ft 5¾ in)

80 mm (3¼ in)

90 mm (3½ in)

60 mm (2¼ in)

450 mm (1 ft 5¾ in)

60 mm (2¼ in)

680 mm (2 ft 3 in)

FRONT VIEW

4 x 400 mm x 20 mm x 20 mm
  (1 ft 3¾ in x ¾ in x ¾ in) pieces oak
  for mouldings on inside of frame
  (or ready-made equivalent)
1 x 412 mm x 400 mm x 16 mm
  (1 ft 4 in x 1 ft 3¾ in x ½ in) piece
  chipboard for seat
2 x 216 mm x 400 mm x 20 mm
  (8¼ in x 1 ft 3¾ in x ¾ in) pieces oak
  for sides of cabinet
2 x 400 mm x 400 mm x 20 mm
  (1 ft 3¾ in x 1 ft 3¾ in x ¾ in) pieces
  oak for top and bottom of cabinet
1 x 372 mm x 400 mm x 20 mm
  (1 ft 2½ in x 1 ft 3¾ in x ¾ in) oak for
  cabinet shelf
1 x 360 mm x 90 mm x 20 mm
  (1 ft 2 in x 3½ in x ¾ in) piece oak for
  drawer face
2 x 350 mm x 90 mm x 15 mm
  (1 ft 1¾ in x 3½ in x ½ in) pieces pine
  for sides of drawer
1 x 360 mm x 70 mm x 15 mm
  (1 ft 2 in x 2¾ in x ½ in) piece pine for
  back of drawer
1 x 378 mm x 334 mm x 7 mm
  (1 ft 3 in x 1 ft 1⅜ in x ½ in) piece
  pine plywood for bottom of drawer
1 x 372 mm x 334 mm x 7 mm
  (1 ft 2 in x 1 ft 1 in x ¼ in) piece pine
  plywood for back of cabinet
16 (38 mm/1½ in x no. 8) countersunk
  screws
Woodworking adhesive
Handle or knob for drawer
Sandpaper
Varnish

Frame for seat

1. First saw and plane the seat frame
to measure.

2. Mark-off the joints (*see* figure 1).

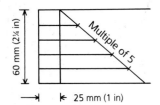

FIG. 1

3. Mark-off the waste wood, then saw
and chisel the joints (*see* figure 2).

Legs

4. Saw and plane the legs to measure.

5. Now mark-off the joints. The bottom
joints must correspond with those of the
seat frame. Saw out half the thickness at
the top of the uprights where they will be

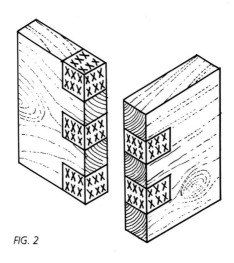

FIG. 2

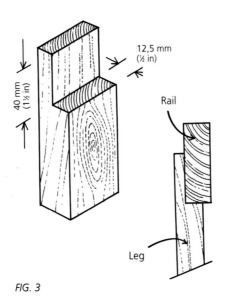

FIG. 3

joined to the inside of the seat frame
(as shown in figure 3).

6. Saw and chisel the joints.

Framework

7. Sand the parts for the frame and the
legs, and glue and cramp these parts.

8. Screw the mouldings to the inside of
the seat frame. Ensure that there is equal
space above and below the mouldings
(*see* figure 4).

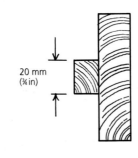

FIG. 4

Cabinet

9. Now saw and plane the boards for the
cabinet to measure.

10. The sides fit into corner rebates in the
top and bottom of the cabinet. The
rebates must be the width of the sides and
two-thirds the thickness of the top and
bottom. Mark-off the rebates, and saw
and chisel them out.

11. The shelf fits into the sides with the
aid of housing joints. Mark-off and make
the housings (*see* illustration in Housing
joints, page 12). Saw out the corners of
the shelf.

12. Sand the parts of the cabinet.

13. Glue and cramp the cabinet. It must fit
loosely into the seat frame.

14. Cut a rebate in the back piece of the
cabinet using a router.

15. Cut the back piece to measure and
place it in position (*see* figure 5).

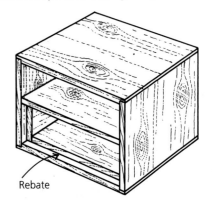

FIG. 5

Drawer

16. Make the drawer (*see* Drawer
construction, page 15).

17. Attach the handle or knob (*see*
Catches and handles, page 19).

Seat

18. Saw the chipboard for the seat to
measure so that it fits into the seat frame.
If you wish, add a cushion (*see* note in the
introduction to this project on page 29).

Finishing and polishing

19. Give all the parts a final sanding and
fill in any small holes in the wood.

20. Varnish the telephone table (*see*
Polishing, page 19).

MAGAZINE RACK

If you have a growing pile of magazines that you would like to store, this rack is ideal for keeping them tidily in one place. Your guests will also enjoy paging through your collection.

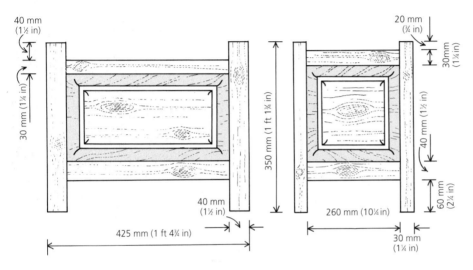

40 mm (1½ in)

30 mm (1¼ in)

FRONT VIEW

425 mm (1 ft 4¾ in)

40 mm (1½ in)

350 mm (1 ft 1¾ in)

20 mm (¾ in)

30 mm (1¼ in)

40 mm (1½ in)

60 mm (2¼ in)

260 mm (10¼ in)

30 mm (1¼ in)

SIDE VIEW

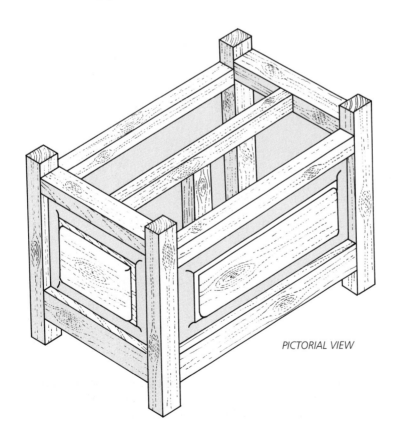

PICTORIAL VIEW

A hardwood can be used for this project for example oak, or preferably beech.

Materials
4 x 350 mm x 40 mm x 30 mm
(1 ft 1¾ in x 1½ in x 1¼ in) pieces beech for legs
2 x 234 mm x 40 mm x 30 mm
(9 in x 1½ in x 1¼ in) pieces beech for top cross-rails
2 x 234 mm x 40 mm x 40 mm
(9 in x 1½ in x 1½ in) pieces beech for bottom cross-rails
2 x 395 mm x 30 mm x 30 mm
(1 ft 3½ in x 1¼ in x 1¼ in) pieces beech for top length rails
2 x 395 mm x 40 mm x 30 mm
(1 ft 3½ in x 1½ in x 1¼ in) pieces beech for bottom length rails
1 x 345 mm x 40 mm x 30 mm
(1 ft 1¾ in x 1½ in x 1¼ in) piece beech for horizontal part of divider
2 x 215 mm x 40 mm x 30 mm
(8½ in x 1½ in x 1¼ in) pieces beech for vertical parts of divider
1 x 365 mm x 220 mm x 9 mm
(1 ft 2¼ in x 8½ in x ⅜ in) piece plywood for base
2 x 220 mm x 220 mm x 15 mm
(8½ in x 8½ in x ½ in) pieces beech for end panels
2 x 365 mm x 200 mm x 15 mm
(1 ft 2¼ in x 8 in x ¼ in) pieces beech for length panels
Woodworking adhesive
Sandpaper
Varnish

End frames and panels
1. Saw out and plane the legs (or stiles) and the cross-rails to measure.

2. Mark-off the mortise-and-tenon joints (see Mortise-and-tenon joints, page 12). Make 10 mm (⅜ in) deep grooves on the

CONSTRUCTION

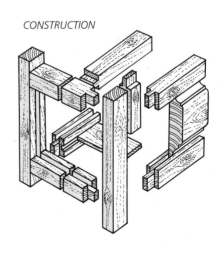

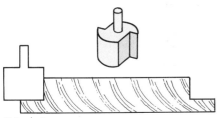
Cut rebate

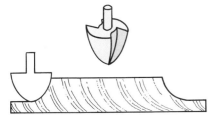
Cut rebate round

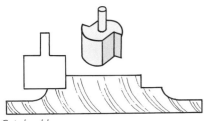
Cut shoulder

Plane edge of panel with a rebate plane
FIG. 1

inside of all parts of the frame, with equal space on either side, for the panels. (*see* construction illustration on page 32.)

3. Now chisel out the mortises and saw the tenons.

4. Plane the grooves on the insides of the frame parts.

5. Saw the wood for the panels to measure, mark-off the inside of the frame and add 10 mm (⅜ in) all around.

6. Cut the shape of the panel with a router. The shape you choose will depend on the bits available (*see* figure 1).

Length rails and panels
7. Saw and plane the wood for the length rails to measure.

8. Mark-off the mortises in the legs (or stiles) of the end frames and the tenons on the length rails. See illustration in figure 2 for explanation.

FIG. 2

9. Chisel out the mortises and saw the tenons (*see* explanation on Mortise-and-tenon joints, page 12).

10. Next, plane grooves on the inside of the length rails and the legs (or stiles). (*see* step 2.)

11. Saw the panels to measure as shown in step 5.

12. Then saw out the shape of the panels (*see* step 6).

Base
13. Plane grooves on the inside of the bottom rails so that the base will fit into them (*see* construction illustration on page 32).

14. Saw the base to measure.

Divider
15. Saw and plane the parts for the divider to measure.

16. Mark-off the mortise-and-tenon joints (*see* Mortise-and-tenon joints, page 12).

17. Chisel out the mortises and saw the tenons. The mortises in the top rail of the end frames must also be chiselled out.

Carcass
18. Sand all the parts.

19. Glue and cramp the end frames around the end panels (*see* Door construction, page 16).

20. Glue and cramp the length rails and panels, the base and the divider between the end frames.

Finishing and polishing
21. Give all the parts a final sanding (*see* Finishing, page 19).

22. Now varnish the completed magazine rack following instructions found in Polishing on page 19.

COFFEE TABLE

A coffee table is a must in every living or family room. This table, with its light construction and pale wood, is suitable for a living room of any size (even a tiny one). You can change the dimensions, if you wish, and use another material for the table top instead of glass.

Oak was used for the project.

Materials
2 x 1 250 mm x 70 mm x 20 mm
  (4 ft 1¼ in x 2¾ in x ¾ in) pieces oak
  for top frame
2 x 660 mm x 70 mm x 20 mm
  (2 ft 2 in x 2¾ in x ¾ in) pieces oak
  for top frame
4 x 430 mm x 50 mm x 50 mm

(1 ft 5 in x 2 in x 2 in) pieces oak
  for legs
2 x 1 180 mm x 60 mm x 20 mm
  (3 ft 10½ in x 2¼ in ¾ in) pieces oak
  for long rails
2 x 590 mm x 60 mm x 20 mm
  (1 ft 11 in x 2¼ in x ¾ in) pieces oak
  for short rails
2 x 1 150 mm x 60 mm x 20 mm
  (3 ft 9 in x 2¼ in x ¾ in) pieces oak

for bottom frame
2 x 560 mm x 60 mm x 20 mm
  (1 ft 10 in x 2¼ in x ¾ in) pieces oak
  for bottom frame
1 x 1 126 mm x 536 mm x 7 mm
  (3 ft 8¾ in x 1 ft 8¾ in x ¼ in) piece
  smoked glass for top frame
1 x 1 046 mm x 456 mm x 7 mm
  (3 ft 5½ in x 1 ft 6 in x ¼ in) piece
  smoked glass for bottom frame
10 fasteners (to secure top frame)
10 countersunk screws (20 mm/¾ in x
  no. 8) to secure fasteners
Woodworking adhesive
Sandpaper
Varnish (preferable when glass is used)

Top frame
1. Saw and plane the wood to measure.

2. Use a concealed corner mortise-and-tenon joint with a mitred shoulder (*see* figure 1) for joining the four parts of the frame. First mark-off and saw the tenon (*see* figure 2). Then saw off the end of the mortise part at an angle of 45°, and mark-off the position of the tenon to determine the position of the mortise (*see* figure 3 for clarification). Chisel out the mortise. Use this method to make all four mortises and tenons for the frame.

3. Plane a rebate at the top inside edge of the four parts of the frame with a rebate plane or router (*see* figure 4). The outside edge of the frame is simply rounded with a router (*see* figure 5).

Bottom frame
4. The size of the bottom frame is equal to the dimensions of the inside of the top frame plus 20 mm (¾ in) on each side. Make the frame according to the measurements given in the list of materials, using the same method as for the top frame.

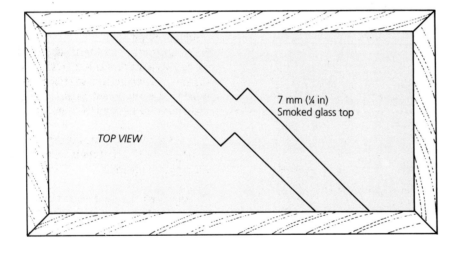

TOP VIEW

7 mm (¼ in)
Smoked glass top

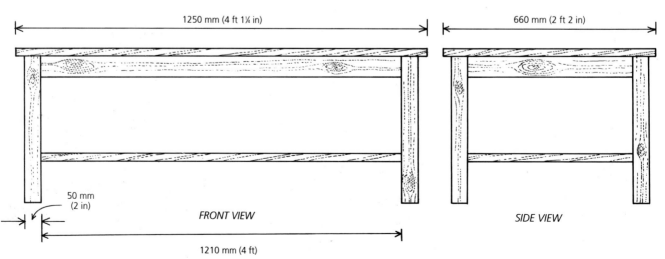

1250 mm (4 ft 1¼ in)

660 mm (2 ft 2 in)

50 mm
(2 in)

FRONT VIEW

SIDE VIEW

1210 mm (4 ft)

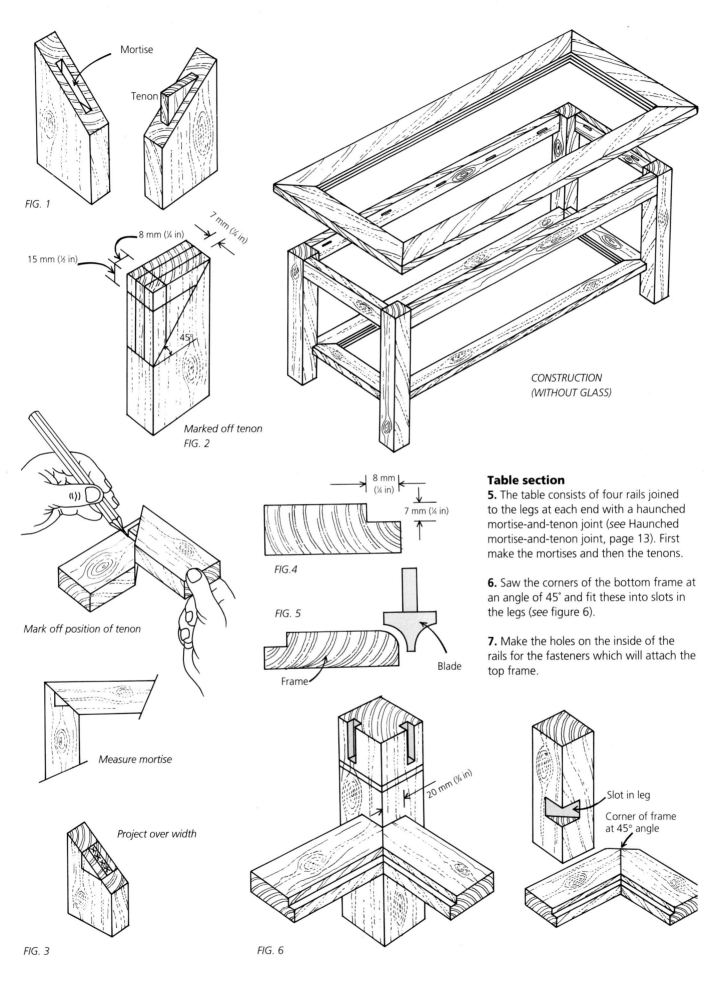

Mortise

Tenon

FIG. 1

8 mm (¼ in)

7 mm (¼ in)

15 mm (½ in)

45°

Marked off tenon
FIG. 2

Mark off position of tenon

Measure mortise

Project over width

FIG. 3

8 mm (¼ in)

7 mm (¼ in)

FIG.4

FIG. 5

Frame

Blade

20 mm (¼ in)

Slot in leg

Corner of frame
at 45° angle

FIG. 6

CONSTRUCTION
(WITHOUT GLASS)

Table section

5. The table consists of four rails joined to the legs at each end with a haunched mortise-and-tenon joint (*see* Haunched mortise-and-tenon joint, page 13). First make the mortises and then the tenons.

6. Saw the corners of the bottom frame at an angle of 45° and fit these into slots in the legs (*see* figure 6).

7. Make the holes on the inside of the rails for the fasteners which will attach the top frame.

8. Now sand all the parts with medium sandpaper of approximately 80 grits before you start glueing. First of all, glue the two length rails between the legs (follow method of construction found in Dining-room table, pages 44-46). Glue and cramp the cross-rails and the lower frame. (*see* construction illustration, page 35).

9. Secure the top frame (which serves as the table top) by screwing in the fasteners (*see* Dining-room table on page 46 for explanation on method).

Finishing and polishing
10. After glueing, sand all the parts again with fine sandpaper (120 grits).

11. Varnish the table (*see* Polishing, page 19).

Inserting the glass
12. When the table is complete, ask a glass dealer to cut the glass to fit and to polish the edges. Usually, the glass rests on flat, round cushions pasted to the wood.

MUSIC CENTRE CABINET

This cabinet has space to house all the units of your music centre and a drawer for compact discs. The space above the doors could be used for knick-knacks or to store more compact discs and tapes.

Veneered chipboard was used for this project, except for the doors and drawer face, which are solid wood. Choose a type of wood that will match the veneer.

Materials
2 x 1 150 mm x 450 mm x 16 mm
(3 ft 9 in x 1 ft 5¾ in x ½ in) pieces
chipboard for sides
4 x 568 mm x 450 mm x 16 mm
(1 ft 10¼ in x 1 ft 5¾ in x ½ in) pieces
chipboard for fixed shelves
1 x 568 mm x 150 mm x 16 mm
(1 ft 10¼ in x 6 in x ½ in) piece
chipboard for base
4 x 566 mm x 45 mm x 20 mm
(1 ft 10¼ in x 1¾ in x ¾ in) pieces solid
wood for door stiles
4 x 244 mm x 45 mm x 20 mm
(9½ in x 1¾ in x ¾ in) pieces solid
wood for door rails
1 x 568 mm x 170 mm x 16 mm
(1 ft 10¼ in x 6¾ in x ½ in) piece
chipboard for drawer face
2 x 480 mm x 208 mm x 4 mm
(1 ft 6¾ in x 8 in x ⅜ in) pieces glass
for door panels
1 x 1 142 mm x 592 mm x 7 mm
(3 ft 9 in x 1 ft 10 in x ¼ in) piece
plywood for back

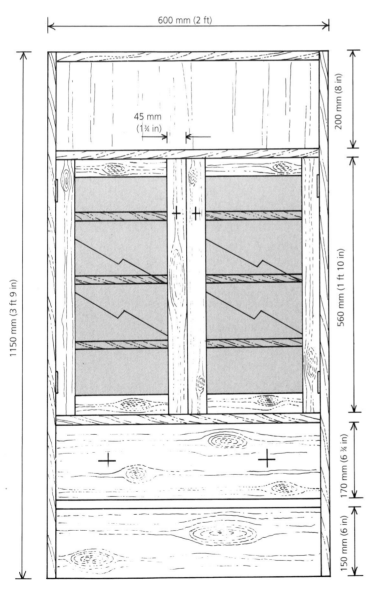

FRONT VIEW

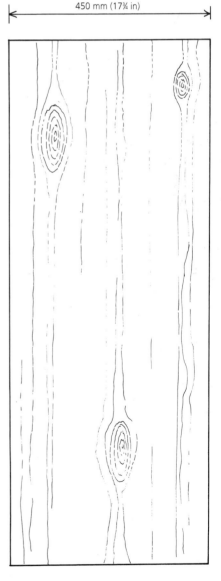

SIDE VIEW

Chipboard screws and plastic plugs to fit screw heads

4 x 50 mm (2 in) brass butt hinges

2 catches for doors

12 x stud shelf supports (see figure 3, Sewing centre, page 83).

Handles for doors and drawer

3 x 568 x 428 mm x 16 mm (1 ft 10¼ in x 1 ft 5 in x ½ in) pieces chipboard for loose shelves (optional)

Construction

1. Ask your dealer to saw all the chipboard to measure and to veneer the edges if the facility is available. Otherwise, veneer the edges by hand yourself.

2. Mark-off the positions for the fixed shelves (two at the top and two at the bottom) and the base on the sides pieces.

3. Drill, and countersink if necessary, the holes for the screws.

4. Screw the fixed shelves to the sides.

5. To make the doors, first saw and plane the stiles and rails to measure. Mark-off and make the joints (see Door construction, page 16). Make the doors to fit between the sides, and the top and bottom fixed shelves, and give them a final sanding. Fix the hinges and hang the doors. Fix the catches.

6. Make the drawer face to fit into the opening between the two bottom fixed shelves. Saw the sides, back piece and bottom pieces of the drawer to size. Mark-off and make the joints (see Drawer construction, page 15). Now assemble the drawer.

7. Mark-off the positions for the loose shelves on the sides and hammer in the stud shelf supports (see Sewing centre, page 83). Slide in the loose shelves.

8. Saw the back piece to measure and secure it to the cabinet with screws. If necessary, you may wish to cut a slot in the back section to pass through the cables of the electrical equipment in the music centre.

9. Give all the parts a final sanding as explained in Finishing on page 19.

10. Attach the handles to the doors and drawer. (For further explanation see Catches and handles on page 19)

11. Varnish the cabinet with your choice of finish. (see Polishing, page 19).

FRONT VIEW

CONSTRUCTION

WALL CABINET

This wall cabinet is ideal for displaying ornaments, such as precious Delft plates, and is best suited for a dining-room. It not only is a beautiful piece of furniture, but is also functional in that it allows you to make optimum use of wall space.

Oak was used for this project.

Materials
2 x 830 mm x 250 mm 20 mm (2 ft 8¾ in x 10 in x ¾ in) pieces oak for sides
1 x 736 mm x 250 mm x 20 mm (2 ft 5 in x 10 in x ¾ in) piece oak for top of cabinet
1 x 724 mm x 250 mm x 20 mm (2 ft 4½ in x 10 in x ¾ in) piece oak for bottom shelf (below cabinet)
1 x 724 mm x 230 mm x 20 mm (2 ft 4½ in x 10 in x ¾ in) piece oak for top shelf of cabinet
1 x 724 mm x 170 mm x 20 mm (2 ft 4½ in x 6¾ in x ¾ in) piece for bottom shelf of cabinet
4 x 450 mm x 50 mm x 20 mm (1 ft 5¾ in x 2 in x ¾ in) pieces oak for door stiles
2 x 350 mm x 50 mm x 20 mm (1 ft 1¾ in x 2 in x ¾ in) pieces oak for top door rails
2 x 350 mm x 60 mm x 20 mm (1 ft 1¾ in x 2¼ in x ¾ in) pieces oak for bottom door rails
2 x 360 mm x 260 mm x 4 mm (1 ft 2 in x 10¼ in x ⅛ in) pieces glass for door panes
Wooden strip to hold glass (beading)
1 x 1 200 mm x 100 mm x 38 mm (4 ft x 4 in x 1½ in) piece oak for crown moulding (or ready-made equivalent)
1 x 736 mm x 464 mm x 7 mm (2 ft 5 in x 1 ft 6½ in x ¼ in) piece plywood for back of cabinet
2 door catches (or sliding catch and lock)
4 x 50 mm (2 in) brass butt hinges
2 doorknobs or handles
2 wall brackets (to hang cabinet on wall)
Tracing paper
Woodworking adhesive
Sandpaper
Varnish or furniture oil

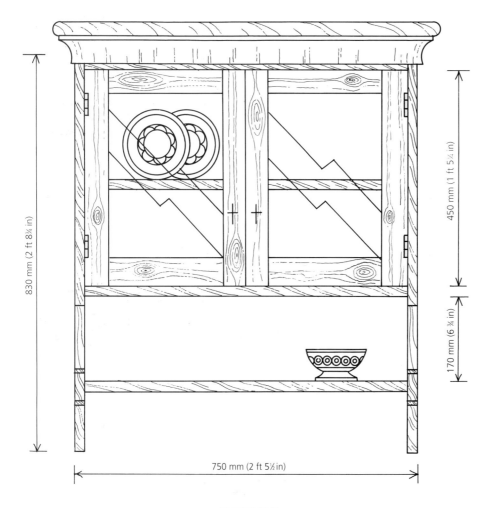

830 mm (2 ft 8¾ in)

750 mm (2 ft 5½ in)

FRONT VIEW

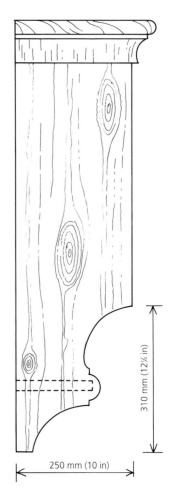

450 mm (1 ft 5¾ in)

170 mm (6 ¾ in)

310 mm (12¼ in)

250 mm (10 in)

SIDE VIEW

Sides

1. First saw and plane the sides of the cabinet to measure.

2. Draw the shape of the sides on a sheet of paper. The shape shown in the illustration, as part of the side view, is on a scale of 1:10 (so enlarge it 10 times to achieve the right size). You could, of course, design your own shape. Use tracing paper to transfer the shape on to the wood.

3. Saw the shape with a jig saw, or with a bow saw or fret saw if you are using hand tools. Finish the shape with files, scrapers and sandpaper.

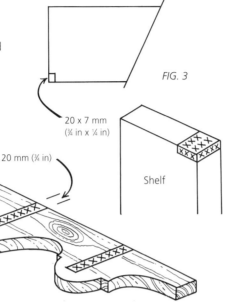

FIG. 1

20 mm (¾ in)

20 mm (¾ in)

4. Mark-off the position of the housings for the shelves (see figure 1). Make sure that the ends of the shelves will fit between the lines you have marked.

5. Now cut the housings with a router, or saw and chisel them out (see Housing joints, page 12).

Top and shelves
6. Saw and plane the top of the cabinet and the shelves to measure. Remember that the top of the cabinet must be longer than the shelves.

7. Mark-off the dovetails for the top of the cabinet (see figure 2 below and Drawer construction, page 16).

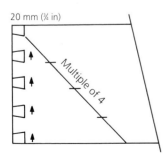

20 mm (¾ in)

Multiple of 4

FIG. 2

8. Saw and chisel out the dovetails.

9. Trace the dovetails from the top of the cabinet on to the end grain of the sides.

10. Saw and chisel out the sockets in the sides.

11. Mark-off the blind corners on the three shelves (see figure 3).

FIG. 3

20 x 7 mm
(¾ in x ¼ in)

20 mm (¾ in)

Shelf

12. Saw out the blind corners.

Carcass
13. Sand the sides, top and shelves, ready for assembly.

FIG. 4

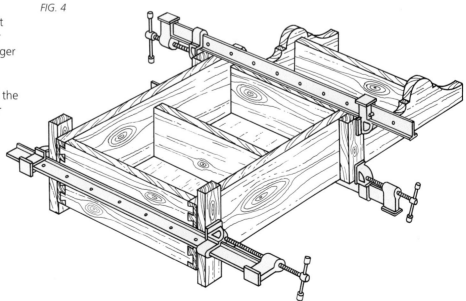

14. Plane rebates in the sides and shelves to house the plywood back piece (see figure 8, page 42).

15. Glue and cramp the carcass (refer to figure 4 for explanation).

Doors
16. Saw and plane the stiles, and top and bottom rails, for the door to measure.

17. Mark-off the joints for the doors (see Door construction, page 16).

18. Make the joints for the door carcass.

19. Sand the parts, then glue and cramp the carcass.

20. Mount the glass in the doors, using a wooden strip (see figure 5).

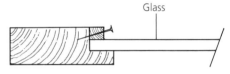

Glass

FIG. 5

21. Fix the hinges to the doors and hang the doors (see Hinges, page 18). Fix the door catches, and attach the door knobs or handles.

Crown moulding
22. You can buy a ready-made crown moulding, or make one yourself from a piece of oak. Adjust the shape according to the bits that you have for your router.

23. Cut the ends at an angle of 45° to fit the top of the cabinet, with allowance made for an overlap. Glue around the top of the cabinet and attach the moulding (*see* figure 6).

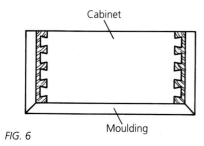

Cabinet

Moulding

FIG. 6

24. Alternatively, you can screw the crown moulding to the cabinet with wooden brackets (*see* figure 7).

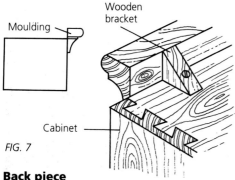

Moulding

Wooden bracket

Cabinet

FIG. 7

Back piece
25. The back piece (of plywood) fits into the rebate in the sides and shelves (*see* figure 8). Screw it into the rebate so that it can be removed if necessary.

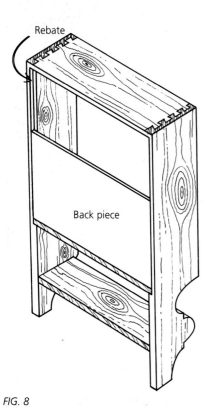

Rebate

Back piece

FIG. 8

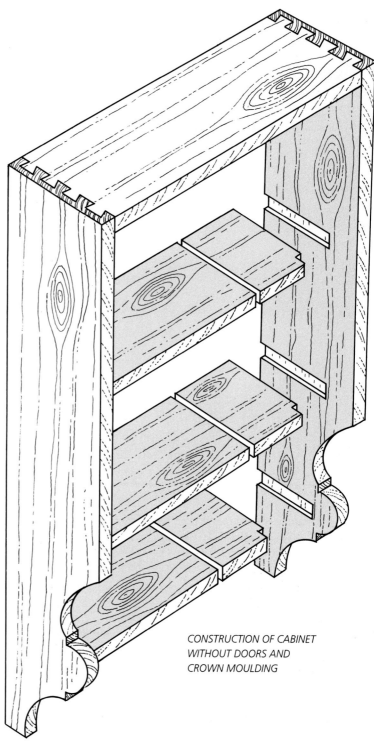

CONSTRUCTION OF CABINET WITHOUT DOORS AND CROWN MOULDING

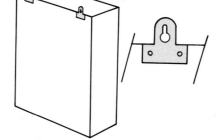

FIG. 9

Wall brackets
26. Screw two wall brackets (shown in figure 9) on to the back of the top shelf. Hook these brackets over two screws which have been fixed into the wall for hanging the cabinet.

Finishing and polishing
27. Give the cabinet a final sanding with fine sandpaper (120 grits).

28. Now finish off the cabinet by polishing with varnish or oil (refer to Polishing, page 19, for further explanation).

DINING-ROOM TABLE

A table is a basic requirement in a dining-room so it is probably one of the first pieces of furniture most people buy when they furnish their home. Don't let the size of this project put you off – with the right tools and these instructions you can make your own dining-room table from solid wood. The rectangular shape of the table is practical as it takes up the least space and can be positioned in more than one way. The table seats eight people. However, the basic construction (carcass) can be adapted to suit various styles and sizes. For example, although very attractive, legs turned on a lathe are not essential, so choose one of the simple alternative styles if you don't have a lathe.

Oregon pine, which is relatively inexpensive, was used for this project. Other types of wood, like oak, can also be used.

Materials

4 x 750 mm x 100 mm x 100 mm
  (2 ft 5½ in x 4 in x 4 in) pieces
  Oregon pine for legs
2 x 750 mm x 120 mm x 30 mm
  (2 ft 5½ in x 4¾ in x 1¼ in) pieces
  Oregon pine for length rails
2 x 1 660 mm x 120 mm x 30 mm
  (5 ft 5½ in x 4¾ in x 1¼ in) pieces
  Oregon pine for cross-rails
1 x 1 800 mm x 900 mm x 30 mm
  (6 ft x 3 ft x 1¼ in) piece glued up
  Oregon pine for table top
1 x 775 mm x 120 mm x 30 mm
  (2 ft 6½ in x 4¾ in x 1¼ in) piece
  Oregon pine for cross-rails under
  table top
16 fasteners to secure top
32 (30 mm/ 1¼ in x no. 8) countersunk
  screws (to fix fasteners)
Woodworking adhesive
Sandpaper
Varnish or furniture oil

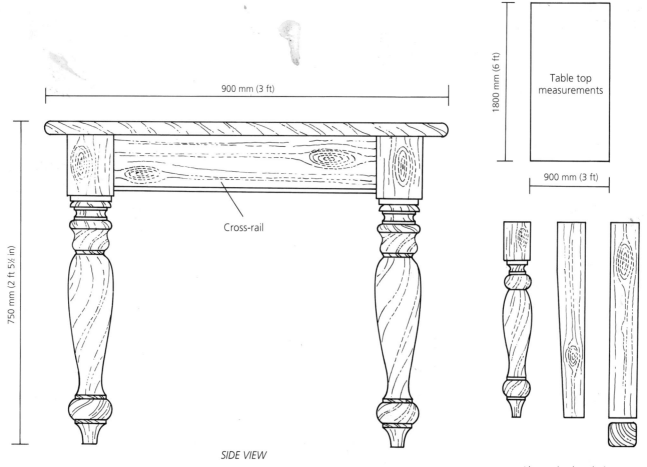

900 mm (3 ft)

750 mm (2 ft 5½ in)

Cross-rail

SIDE VIEW

1800 mm (6 ft)

Table top measurements

900 mm (3 ft)

Alternative leg designs

1. Plane all the wood to measure before you begin with the construction.

Legs

2. If you are turning the legs on a lathe, first mark them off to fit inside a rectangle measuring 750 mm x 100 mm (2 ft 5½ in x 4 in) – (see figure 1).

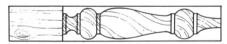

FIG. 1

3. Turn the leg on the lathe (see Turning a table leg, page 17).

4. Mark-off the positions of the mortises for the mortise-and-tenon joints. First determine the position where the rail will join the leg (see figure 2). Using a double-point gauge, mark-off the middle third of the rail thickness (or the closest chisel width to it) from the point where the rail will join the leg (see Mortise-and-tenon

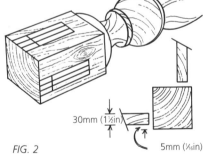

30mm (1½in)   5mm (⅛in)

FIG. 2

joints, page 12). Give the tenon a shoulder or haunch of about 25 mm (1 in); in other words, the mortise does not run to the full length of the leg.

5. Now chisel out the mortises (if necessary, refer to Mortise-and-tenon joints on page 12 for help).

6. Saw and chisel the haunched part of the joint (see figure 3).

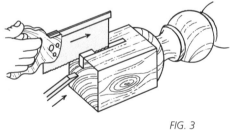

FIG. 3

Rails

7. Saw length and cross-rails to measure.

8. Mark-off the tenons (see Haunched mortise-and-tenon joint, page 13). Each tenon must be 60 mm (2¼ in) long and the thickness must be the same as that of the mortise (about one-third of the thickness of the wood).

9. Saw the tenons.

10. The cross-rail in the middle of the table must fit into two housing joints in

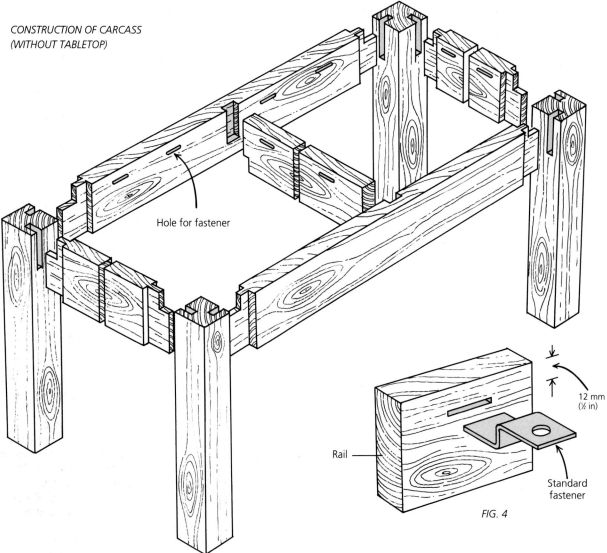

Hole for fastener

Rail

12 mm
(½ in)

Standard
fastener

FIG. 4

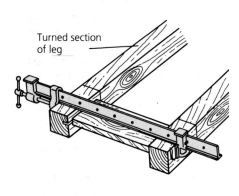

Turned section
of leg

FIG. 5

the length rails. Mark-off the housings, then saw and chisel out (*see* Housing joints, page 12).

Cramping the carcass

11. The construction illustration above shows how to assemble the carcass for the table. First make the holes for the top's

fasteners before you glue the carcass. You may chisel out the holes as for a mortise-and-tenon joint (*see* figure 4), if you wish.

12. Figure 5 illustrates how the table is cramped. Remember to finish sanding all the carcass parts before glueing them. Loosely glue and cramp the legs with the cross-rails between them, and then with the length rails between them.

Glueing the table top

13. Plane the table top boards to thickness and plane all the edges square and true. Next, glue the edges (*see* Edge joints, page 14). Plane and sand the top until it is completely level and smooth. Now saw the table top to measure and finish off the edges neatly with a router (*see* page 9 for information on power routers).

14. Screw the completed table top to the carcass with some of the fasteners. Refer to the illustration in figure 6 for method of attaching fasteners.

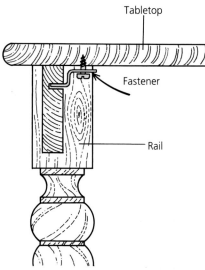

Tabletop

Fastener

Rail

FIG. 6

Finishing and polishing

15. Give the table a final sanding with fine sandpaper (at least 120 grits).

16. Polish the table with oil or varnish (*see* Polishing, page 19).

COCKTAIL CABINET/ SERVING TROLLEY

This double-purpose unit has storage space for wine and it serves as a trolley to bring drinks to your guests. It forms a unit when the trolley is pushed into the corner of the fixed component. The bottle rack fits into the cabinet, or it can be used separately.

Oak, melamine chipboard, plain chipboard and cork tiles were used for this project.

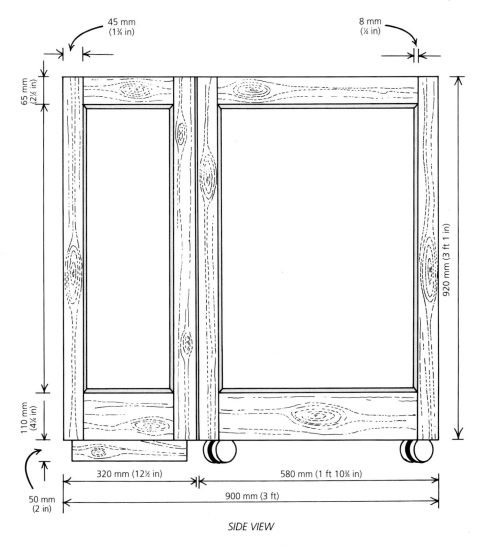

SIDE VIEW

45 mm (1¾ in)

8 mm (¼ in)

65 mm (2½ in)

920 mm (3 ft 1 in)

110 mm (4¼ in)

50 mm (2 in)

320 mm (12½ in)

580 mm (1 ft 10¾ in)

900 mm (3 ft)

Materials

Cabinet

6 x 870 mm x 45 mm x 45 mm (2 ft 10¼ in x 1¾ in x 1¾ in) pieces oak for frame stiles

2 x 880 mm x 65 mm x 20 mm (2 ft 10¾ in x 2½ in x ¾ in) pieces oak for top outer rails

2 x 560 mm x 65 mm x 20 mm (1 ft 10 in x 2½ in x ¾ in) pieces oak for top inner rails

2 x 300 mm x 65 mm x 20 mm (12 in x 2½ in x ¾ in) pieces oak for top side rails

2 x 880 mm x 110 mm x 20 mm (2 ft 10¾ in x 4½ in x ¾ in) pieces oak for bottom outer rails

2 x 560 mm x 110 mm x 20 mm (1 ft 10 in x 4¼ in x ¾ in) pieces oak for bottom inner rails

2 x 300 mm x 110 mm x 20 mm (12 in x 4¼ in x ¾ in) pieces oak for bottom side rails

2 x 695 mm x 230 mm x 16 mm (2 ft 3¼ in x 9 in x ½ in) pieces cream-coloured melamine chipboard for narrow side panels

2 x 695 mm x 810 mm x 16 mm (2 ft 3¼ in x 2 ft 7¾ in x ½ in) pieces cream-coloured melamine chipboard for wide side panels (back of unit)

2 x 860 mm x 860 mm x 16 mm (2 ft 10 in x 2 ft 10 in x ½ in) pieces cream-coloured melamine chipboard for shelf and bottom

1 x 860 mm x 860 mm x 16 mm (2 ft 10 in x 2 ft 10 in x ½ in) piece plain chipboard for top

6 x 280 mm x 20 mm x 20 mm (11 in x ¾ in x ¾ in) pieces moulding for shelf, top and bottom to rest on

6 x 820 mm x 20 mm x 20 mm (2 ft 10¼ in x ¾ in x ¾ in) strips wood for top, shelf and bottom to rest on

6 x 560 mm x 20 mm x 20 mm (1 ft 10 in x ¾ in x ¾ in) strips wood for top, shelf and bottom to rest on

2 x 860 mm x 70 mm x 20 mm (2 ft 10 in x 2¾ in x ¾ in) pieces oak for base

2 x 280 mm x 70 mm x 20 mm (11 in x 2¾ in x ¾ in) pieces oak for base

2 x 600 x 70 mm x 20 mm (2 ft 2¾ in x ¾ in) pieces oak for base

4 x 870 mm x 12 mm x 8 mm (2 ft 10¼ in x ½ in x ⅜ in) pieces beading for rebate inside frame

4 x 230 mm x 12 mm x 8 mm (9 in x ½ in x ⅜ in) cork tiles for top

Woodworking adhesive

Sandpaper

Varnish

Contact glue

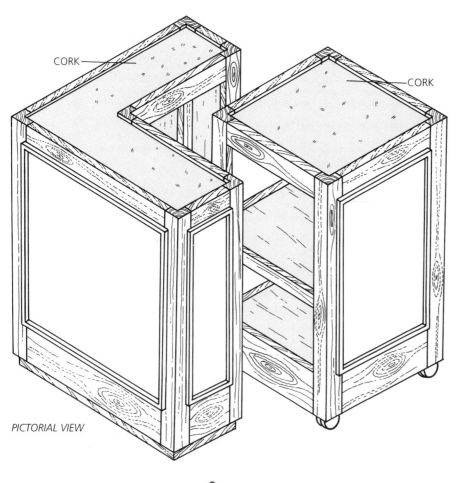

CORK

CORK

PICTORIAL VIEW

Serving trolley

4 x 870 mm x 45 mm x 45 mm
(2 ft 10¼ in x 1¾ in x 1¾ in) pieces oak
for stiles for side frames

4 x 540 mm x 65 mm x 20 mm (1 ft 9 in
x 2½ in x ¾ in) pieces oak for top rails

4 x 540 mm x 110 mm x 20 mm
(1 ft 9 in x 4¼ in x ¾ in) pieces oak for
bottom rails

2 x 695 mm x 490 mm x 16 mm
(2 ft 3¼ in x 1 ft 7¼ in x ½ in) pieces
cream-coloured melamine chipboard
for panels

12 x 490 mm x 20 mm x 20 mm
(1 ft 7¼ in x ¾ in x ¾ in) strips wood
for top, shelf and bottom to rest on

2 x 490 mm x 490 mm x 16 mm
(1 ft 7¼ in x 1 ft 7¼ in x ½ in) pieces
cream-coloured melamine chipboard
for shelf and bottom

1 x 490 mm x 490 mm x 16 mm
(1 ft 7¼ in x 1 ft 7¼ in x ½ in) piece
plain chipboard for top

4 x 695 mm x 12 mm x 8 mm
(1 ft 3¼ in x ½ in x ⅜ in) pieces
beading for rebates

4 x 495 mm x 12 mm x 8 mm
(1 ft 3¼ in x ½ in x ⅜ in) pieces beading to create rebates

4 small castors

Cork tiles for top

Woodworking adhesive

Contact glue

Sandpaper

Varnish

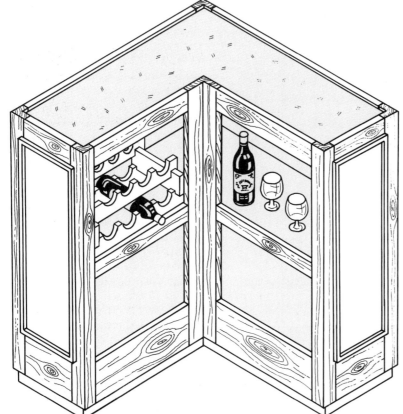

SOLID SECTION OF UNIT WITH STORAGE AREA FOR WINE AND GLASSES

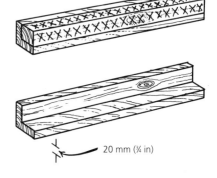

20 mm (¾ in)

FIG. 1

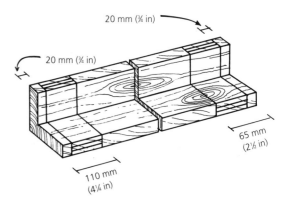

20 mm (¾ in)

20 mm (¾ in)

65 mm
(2½ in)

110 mm
(4¼ in)

Construction

1. Saw out corners of the stiles, using a circular saw (*see* figure 1).

2. Mark-off the mortises for the side rails (*see* figure 2).

3. Chisel out the mortises (*see* Mortise-and-tenon joints, page 12).

4. Saw and plane the top and bottom rails to measure.

5. Mark-off the tenons (*see* figure 3).

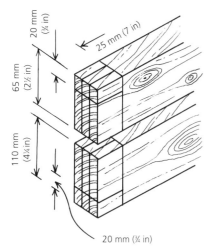

FIG. 2

6. Saw the tenons (*see* Mortise-and-tenon joints, page 12).

7. Sand, glue and cramp the frames for one side (*see* figure 4).

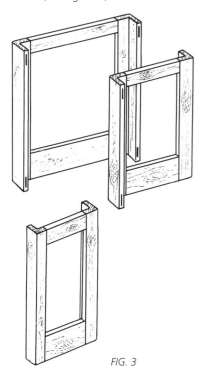

FIG. 3

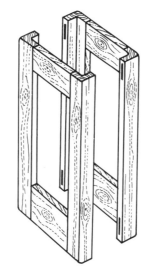

FIG. 4

8. Secure beading by nailing in the frames that have been glued, to form a rebate for the panels (*see* figures 5 and 6).

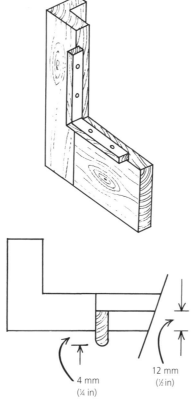

FIG. 5

9. Saw the panels exactly to measure so that they will fit correctly into the rebate side of the frames.

10. Saw a rebate on the inside of the panels to secure them (*see* figure 6).

11. Secure the panels with the melamine on the outside (*see* figure 6).

12. Glue the rails of the other sides between the completed frames.

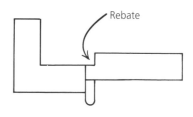

Rebate

Secured panel

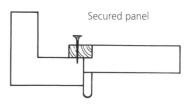

FIG. 6

13. Secure the beadings of the frames for the side panels as before.

14. Plane the panels for the frames to measure, cut their rebates and secure.

15. Fix the beading on the insides of the frames for the top, shelf and bottom to rest on. These must be glued to the insides of the rails (*see* figure 7).

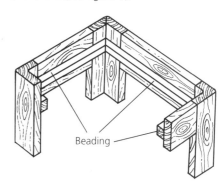

Beading

FIG. 7

16. Saw the tops, shelves and bottoms to measure and glue to the beading.

17. Saw the wood for the base of the fixed unit and saw the corners at an angle of 45° (*see* figure 8, page 51).

18. Screw the base to the inside of the framework (*see* figure 9, page 51).

19. Fix the castors to the bottom of the trolley. The attachment method will depend on the kind of castors you are using. (Ask your hardware dealer for advice). Remember that the height of the base of the cabinet and the height of the castors on the trolley must be the same.

mitre

FIG. 8

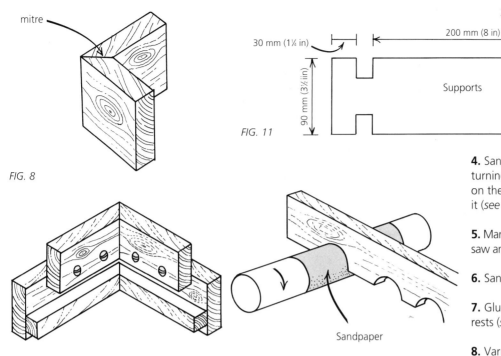

30 mm (1¼ in)   200 mm (8 in)   20 mm (¾ in)

90 mm (3½ in)   Supports   50 mm (2 in)

FIG. 11

4. Sand the hollows either by hand, or by turning a cylinder with the same diameter on the lathe and pasting sandpaper on to it (*see* figure 10).

5. Mark-off housings in the supports, then saw and chisel them out (*see* figure 11).

6. Sand all the parts.

7. Glue the supports between the bottle rests (*see* illustration below).

8. Varnish the bottle rack (*see* Polishing, page 19).

FIG. 9

FIG. 10

Sandpaper

20. Cut the cork tiles to fit the top of the cabinet. Leave them for a day to stretch or shrink, then glue to the surface with contact glue. Make sure they fit snugly against each other.

21. Sand all wooden parts (lightly sand the cork as well), using fine sandpaper.

22. Varnish the finished trolley (*see* Polishing, page 19).

Bottle rack

Materials
4 x 420 mm x 70 mm x 20 mm
(1 ft 4½ in x 2¾ in x ¾ in) pieces oak
for cross-bars (bottle rests)
4 x 300 mm x 90 mm x 20 mm
(12 in x 3½ in x ¾ in) pieces oak
for supports
Woodworking adhesive
Sandpaper
Varnish

Construction
1. Saw and plane the cross-bars of the bottle rack to measure.

2. Mark-off the positions of the semi-circular hollows which will hold the bottles. Note that the front hollows have a diameter of 35 mm (1¼ in) and the back hollows a diameter of 80 mm (3½ in). Draw these curves with a pencil compass.

3. Saw out the hollows using either a jig saw or band saw.

30 mm (1¼ in)

80 mm (3½ in)

70 mm (2¾ in)

35 mm (1½ in)

Measurements of cross-bar

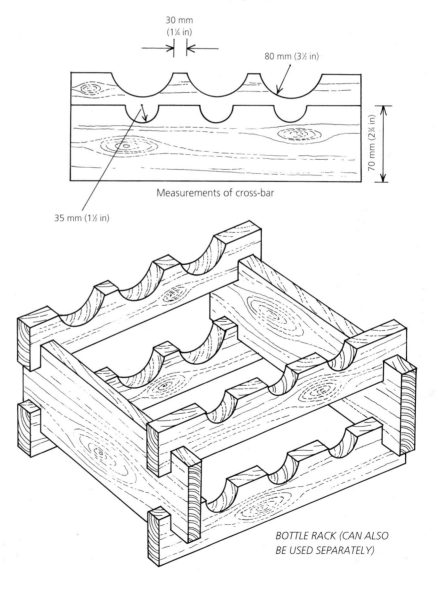

BOTTLE RACK (CAN ALSO BE USED SEPARATELY)

DISPLAY CABINET

A practical and attractive piece of furniture, this cabinet has display space on the shelves and storage space below. To make it even more useful, attach cup hooks for hanging cups and mugs.

Solid oak was used for this cabinet.

Materials
2 x 1 610 mm x 500 mm x 20 mm
   (5 ft 4 in x 1 ft 7½ in x ¾ in) pieces
   oak for sides
2 x 574 mm x 500 mm x 20 mm
   (1 ft 10½ in x 1 ft 7½ in x ¾ in) pieces
   oak for two bottom shelves
3 x 574 mm x 300 mm x 20 mm
   (1 ft 10½ in x 12 in x ¾ in) pieces oak
   for three top shelves
1 x 586 mm x 1 610 mm x 7 mm
   (1 ft 11 in x 5 ft 4 in x ¼ in) piece oak
   plywood for back
1 x 574 mm x 100 mm x 20 mm
   (1 ft 10½ in x 4 in x ¾ in) piece oak
   for base
2 x 450 mm x 60 mm x 20 mm
   (1 ft 5¾ in x 2¼ in x ¾ in) pieces oak
   for door stiles
2 x 530 mm x 60 mm x 20 mm
   (1 ft 8¾ in x 2¼ in x ¾ in) pieces oak
   for door rails
1 x 344 mm x 494 mm x 16 mm
   (1 ft 1½ in x 1 ft 7½ in x ½ in) piece
   oak for door panel
Panel pins (to secure back piece)
2 x 50 mm (2 in) brass butt hinges
1 door catch
1 oak doorknob (ready-made or
   turned on a lathe)
12 (20 mm/¾ in x 8) countersunk
   screws
Woodworking adhesive
Sandpaper
Varnish or furniture oil
6 cup hooks (optional)

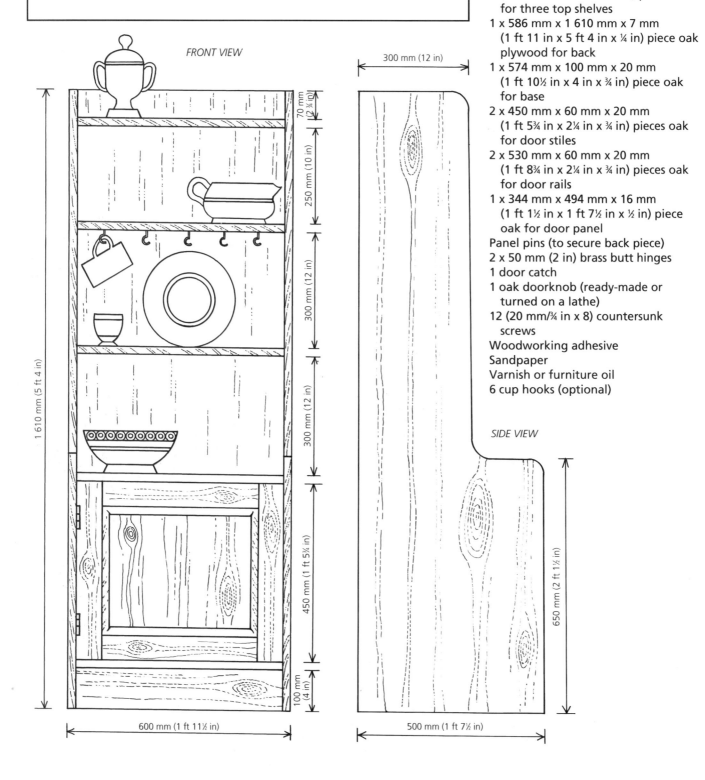

FRONT VIEW

70 mm (2¾ in)

250 mm (10 in)

300 mm (12 in)

300 mm (12 in)

1 610 mm (5 ft 4 in)

450 mm (1 ft 5¾ in)

100 mm (4 in)

600 mm (1 ft 11½ in)

300 mm (12 in)

SIDE VIEW

650 mm (2 ft 1½ in)

500 mm (1 ft 7½ in)

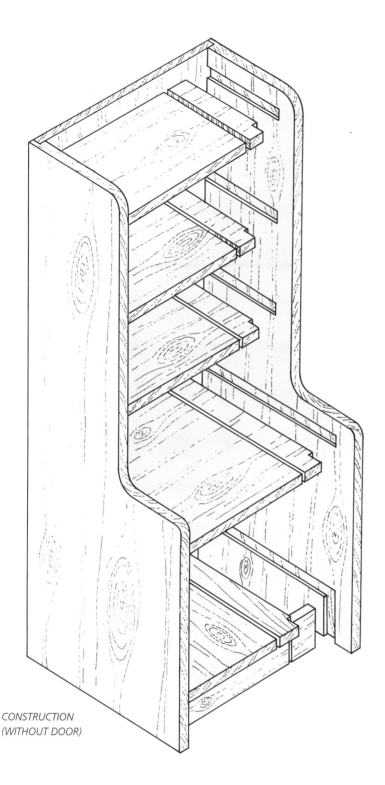

CONSTRUCTION
(WITHOUT DOOR)

housings. Mark-off the corners on the shelves that must be sawn out (*see* Housing joints, page 12).

7. Now make the housings by cutting with a router, or use the method given under the section on Housing joints on page 12. Saw out the corners.

8. Make the housings for the base.

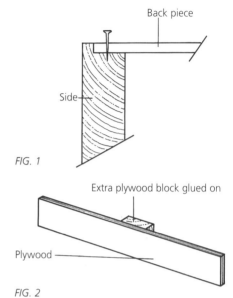

FIG. 1

FIG. 2

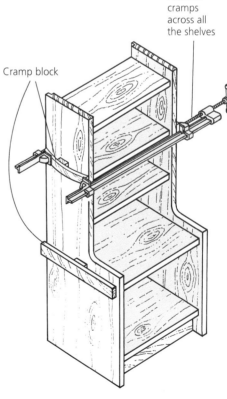

FIG. 3

Glueing the sides
1. First glue the boards for the sides (*see* Edge joints, page 14).

2. Plane and sand the boards until smooth, then saw to measure.

Shaping the sides
3. Draw the shape (*see* illustration of side view) on to the wood and saw it out with a band saw or a jig saw.

4. Finish the sawn edges with a scraper and sandpaper.

Glueing the shelves
5. Glue up the shelf boards, then saw them square and to measure.

Housing joints
6. Determine the positions of the housing joints on the sides and check whether the ends of the shelves fit correctly into the

Planing the rebate
9. Plane two rebates at the back of the sides so that the back piece will fit into them (*see* figure 1).

Cabinet carcass
10. Sand all the parts of the carcass with fine sandpaper (120 grits).

11. Make cramp blocks as shown in figure 2. The blocks will help to pull the full width of the shelves into the housings. Now glue and cramp the carcass (*see* figure 3).

12. Cut the back piece to measure and hammer panel pins into the rebate at the back of the sides to secure.

Door carcass and panel
13. Saw and plane the wood to measure for the door frame: the stiles and rails.

14. Now mark off all the joints and make the door-frame (*see* Door construction, page 16).

15. Glue and cramp the frame (*see* Door construction, page 16).

16. Glue together boards for the panel (in other words, glue the sides of the board to obtain the correct size panel), and plane to measure.

17. Now shape the panel with a router or, alternatively, by hand (*see* Hall stand, page 24, step 20).

18. Fit the panels.

19. Plane the door carcass exactly to measure so that it fits neatly into the cabinet and attach the hinges (*see* Hinges, page 18).

20. Fasten the door catch and attach the doorknob (refer to section on Catches and handles on page 19).

Finishing and polishing
21. For a smooth professional finish, give the completed cabinet a thorough final sanding with fine sandpaper (at least 120 grits).

22. Decide whether you want to varnish or oil the cabinet (*see* Polishing, page 19) and apply your chosen finish.

Cup hooks
23. Cup hooks could be a functional addition to the cabinet. If desired, screw in cup hooks to hang cups and mugs.

VEGETABLE CUTTING BOARD

This simple cutting board makes preparing vegetables and fruit so much easier because the finished items can be scraped into the bowl as you work. It is designed to be used with a bowl 250 mm (10 in) in diameter with a height of 100 mm (4 in). Adjust the dimensions of the board to match the size of the bowl you intend using.

Oak was used for the board.

Materials

1 x 400 mm x 330 mm x 30 mm
(1 ft 3¾ in x 1 ft 1 in x 1¼ in) piece
oak for cutting board

2 x 100 mm x 330 mm x 30 mm
(4 in x 1 ft 1 in x 1¼ in) pieces oak
for supports
Waterproof woodworking adhesive
Sandpaper
Olive oil

Construction

1. Glue together the edges of the wood for the cutting board and the supports (*see* Edging joints, page 14) to obtain the required size.

2. Saw the glued-up boards to measure.

3. Draw a semi-circle at the one end of the cutting board, using the bowl as a guide. Draw a smaller semi-circle running parallel to the first. There should be a space of 10 mm (⅜ in) between the two (*see* the illustration of the view from above).

4. Saw the wood along the smaller curve.

5. Using a router, cut a rebate 10 mm (⅜ in) wide and 10 mm (⅜ in) deep in the bottom of the cutting board, parallel to the sawn-out curve (*see* figure 1).

6. Mark-off and chisel out the housings for the supports (*see* Housing joints, page 12).

7. Glue the supports into the housings.

8. Sand the cutting board.

9. Oil the board regularly with olive oil.

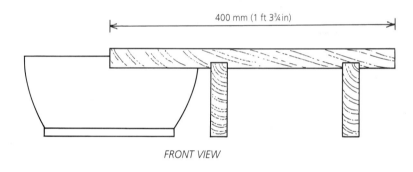

400 mm (1 ft 3¾ in)

FRONT VIEW

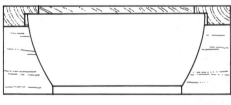

SIDE VIEW

VIEW FROM ABOVE

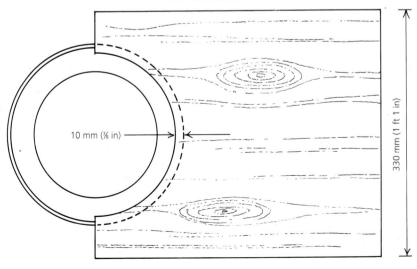

10 mm (⅜ in)

330 mm (1 ft 1 in)

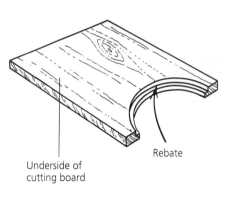

Underside of
cutting board

Rebate

FIG. 1

BATHROOM CABINET

This bathroom cabinet offers considerably more space than the cheaper equivalents available in the shops. It has sufficient space for toiletries, a vanity or shaving mirror, and a towel rail.

Oregon pine was used for the cabinet.

Materials

2 x 760 mm x 220 mm x 20 mm
   (2 ft 6 in x 8½ in x ¾ in) pieces
   Oregon pine for sides
2 x 644 mm x 220 mm x 20 mm
   (2 ft 1¼ in x 8½ in x ¾ in) pieces
   Oregon pine for top and
   bottom shelves

1 x 514 mm x 220 mm x 20 mm
   (1 ft 8¼ x 8½ in x ¾ in) piece
   Oregon pine for vertical divider
2 x 244 mm x 220 mm x 20 mm
   (9¾ in x 8½ in x ½ in) pieces Oregon
   pine for smaller shelves
1 x 644 mm x 100 mm x 20 mm
   (2 ft 1¼ in x 4 in x ¾ in) piece
   Oregon pine for top horizontal rail
2 x 500 mm x 50 mm x 20 mm
   (1 ft 7½ in x 2 in x ¾ in) pieces

Oregon pine for stiles of door frame
2 x 350 mm x 50 mm x 20 mm
   (1 ft 1¾ in x 2 in x ¾ in) pieces
   Oregon pine for rails of
   door frame
1 x 528 mm x 658 mm x 7 mm
   (1 ft 9 in x 2 ft 2 in x ¼ in) Oregon
   pine plank for back piece
1 x 644 mm x 35 mm x 35 mm
   (2 ft 1¼ in x 1½ in x 1½ in) piece
   Oregon pine for towel rail
   (rounded on a lathe or with
   a router)
1 x 414 mm x 264 mm x 4 mm
   (1 ft 4¼ in x 10½ in x ⅜ in) mirror
2 x 50 mm (2 in) brass butt hinges
16 (20 mm/¾ in x 8) countersunk
   screws (to fix hinges and
   wall brackets)
1 Oregon pine wooden knob
   (turned on a lathe or
   ready-made)
Woodworking adhesive
Sandpaper
Varnish or furniture oil
2 mirror brackets

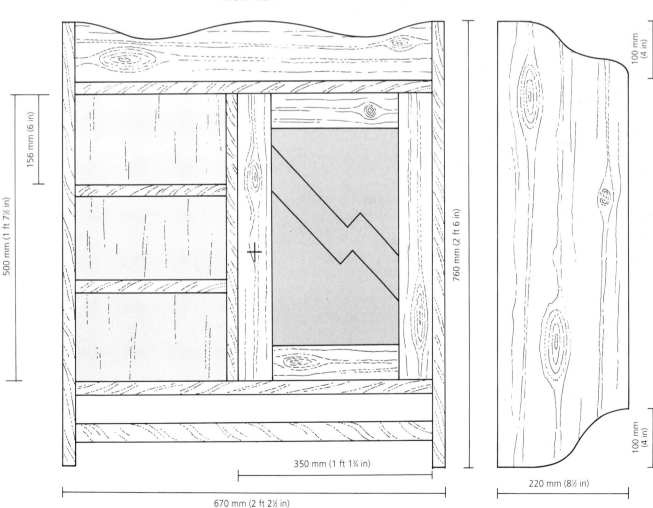

FRONT VIEW

156 mm (6 in)

500 mm (1 ft 7½ in)

760 mm (2 ft 6 in)

350 mm (1 ft 1¾ in)

670 mm (2 ft 2½ in)

SIDE VIEW

100 mm (4 in)

100 mm (4 in)

220 mm (8½ in)

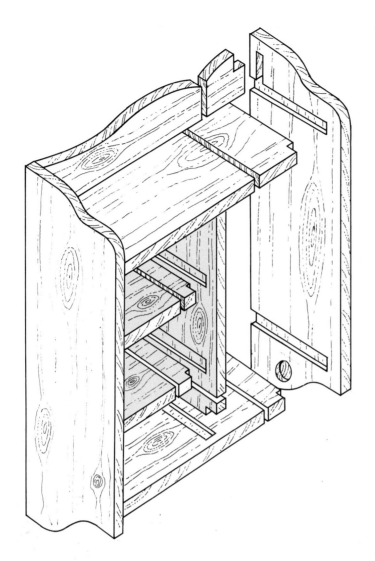

FIG. 1

Sides and vertical divider

1. First saw and plane the sides and divider to measure.

2. Draw the shape of the sides on to the wood (*see* side view illustration found on page 57). Once you are happy with the shape, saw out with a jig saw.

3. Mark-off the position of the housings on the sides and divider.

4. Saw and plane the housings (*see* Housing joints, page 12) on the sides and the divider.

5. Mark-off the position of the holes for the towel rail on the sides and drill to a depth of 14 mm (½ in).

6. Cut the rebates for the back piece in the sides.

Shelves and towel rail

7. First saw and plane all the shelves for both the top and bottom of the cabinet to measure.

8. Now mark off the ends to be sawn o and saw.

9. Mark off the position of the grooves the shelves, then saw and plane.

10. Saw and plane the two smaller mid shelves to measure, then mark-off and saw out the ends.

11. Turn the towel rail on a lathe to a diameter of 30 mm (1½ in).

12. Cut the rebates for the back piece in the bottom and top shelves.

Carcass

13. Sand all the parts of the carcass with fine sandpaper (120 grits).

14. Glue and cramp the top and bottom shelves and also the vertical divider (*see* figure 1 for clarification).

15. Glue the sides under the shelves, the top rail and the towel rail to the glued-up part. (see Wall cabinet, page 40.)

Door carcass

16. Saw and plane the stiles and rails to measure.

17. Make the door carcass (*see* Door construction, page 16), ensuring it is true.

18. Fit the hinges (*see* Hinges, page 18), insert the mirror and hang the door.

Back piece

19. The back piece consists of Oregon pine planks that fit into each other sideways with rebates and are screwed into a rebate (*see* figure 2). Plane the beams to

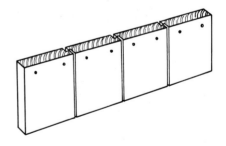

FIG. 2

20. Screw the planks in the right position.

Wall brackets

21. Fix the wall brackets (*see* Wall cabinet, page 42).

Finishing and polishing

22. Give the cabinet a final sanding with fine sandpaper.

23. Varnish the cabinet or polish with oil (*see* Polishing, page 19).

TOWEL RACK

The metal or plastic fittings so frequently found in bathrooms can look cold and clinical. This functional towel rack lends warmth to the room, and you can move it around if you need a change.

Oak was used for the towel rack.

Materials

2 x 310 mm x 70 mm x 20 mm
(12¼ in x 2¾ in x ¾ in) pieces oak
for bottom cross-rails
2 x 250 mm x 70 mm x 20 mm
(10 in x 2¾ in x ¾ in) pieces oak for
top cross-rails

4 x 750 mm x 35 mm x 20 mm
(2 ft 5½ in x 1½ in x ¾ in) pieces
oak for uprights (legs)
5 x 850 mm x 25 mm x 25 mm
(2 ft 10½ in x 1 in x 1 in) pieces oak
for towel rails
Woodworking adhesive
Sandpaper
Varnish

Side frames

1. Shape the top cross-rails. Draw the shape inside a 250 mm x 70 mm (10 in x 2¾ in) rectangle. Draw the curves with a pencil compass. The radius of the lower curve is 160 mm (6¼ in) and that of the top curve 210 mm (8¼ in). The midpoints of the curves are on the centre line (*see* figure 1).

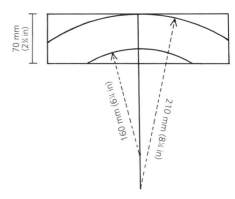

FIG. 1

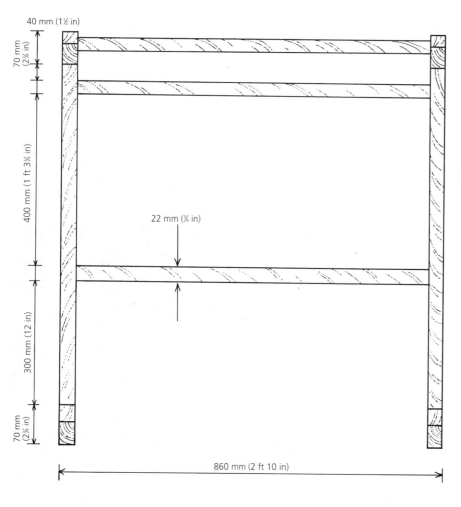

FRONT VIEW

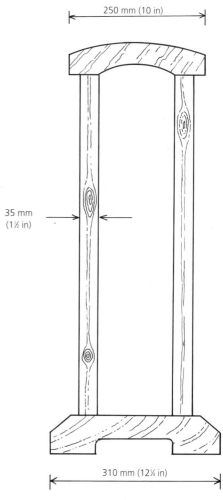

SIDE VIEW

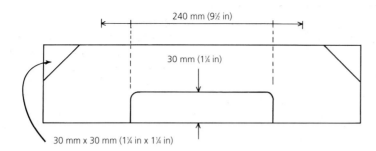

240 mm (9½ in)

30 mm (1¼ in)

FIG. 2

30 mm x 30 mm (1¼ in x 1¼ in)

2. Shape the bottom cross-rails. Draw the shape of the bottom cross-rail to fit into a 310 mm x 70 mm (12¼ in x 2¾ in) rectangle (*see* figure 2).

3. Mark-off the tenons and mortises for the uprights (legs). First, chisel out the mortises in the top and bottom cross-rails, then saw the tenons at each end of the legs (*see* Mortise-and-tenon joints found on page 12). The top tenons must be 15 mm (½ in) and the bottom tenons should be 25 mm (1 in) long.

4. Glue together the side frames. Cramp the frames as for a door (*see* Door construction, page 16). You will need a cramping block for the top cross-rail, which is round. You could use the waste wood piece for this purpose (*see* figure 3).

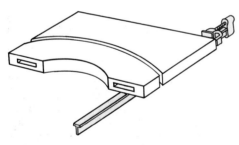

FIG. 3

Towel rails
5. Saw the boards for the towel rails to measure and mark off the tenons at each end while they are still square. The tenons must be 15 mm (½ in) long and extend the full width of the rails (*see* figure 4). Now saw the tenons. Mark-off and chisel out the mortises in the side frames.

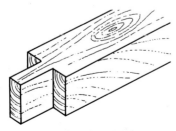

FIG. 4

6. Shape the rails to a round shape with a router (*see* figure 5).

Carcass
7. Sand all the parts with medium sandpaper (100 grits).

8. Glue and cramp the carcass. The cramps must run parallel to the rails.

Finishing and polishing
9. Give the rack a final sanding.

10. Varnish the rack (*see* Polishing, page 19). It is important to use waterproof varnish because damp towels will be hung on the rails.

FIG. 5

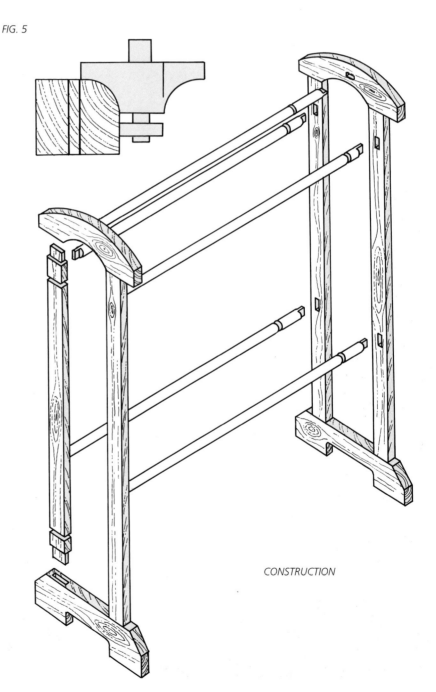

CONSTRUCTION

MIRROR FRAME

Everyone likes to use a full-length mirror from time to time. A separate mirror frame, such as this one, means that you can re-arrange your bedroom furniture as and when you like. Although this frame is made of oak, you could use any wood to match the rest of your furniture.

Materials

2 x 1 600 mm x 70 mm x 20 mm
   (5 ft 3½ in x 2¾ in x ¾ in) pieces
   oak for stiles
2 x 650 mm x 70 mm x 20 mm (2 ft 1½ in
   x 2¾ in x ¾ in) pieces oak for rails
1 x 1 510 mm x 560 mm x 7 mm
   (4 ft 11½ in x 1 ft 10 in x ¼ in) piece
   plywood for back piece
1 x 1 480 mm x 530 mm x 7 mm
   (4 ft 10 in x 1 ft 8¾ in x ¼ in) mirror
Woodworking adhesive
2 mirror brackets
Piece of thin foam rubber (optional)
Sandpaper
Varnish

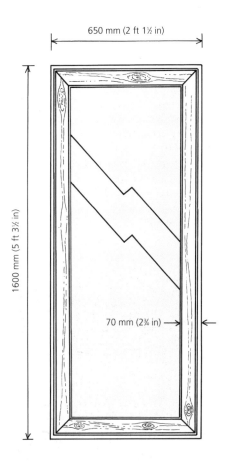

650 mm (2 ft 1½ in)

1600 mm (5 ft 3½ in)

70 mm (2¾ in)

FRONT VIEW

piece. You could place a thin layer of packing sponge rubber between the two to hold the mirror securely in place.

3. Once the frame is complete and the rebates have been cut, saw the back piece to measure. As a temporary measure, screw the back piece into the rebate in which it must fit.

4. Decorate the outer and inner edges of the frame with a router if you wish (*see* figure 2).

5. Fix two mirror brackets (two-thirds from the bottom) to the mirror frame so that it

can be hung on the wall (*see* figure 3). Drill a hole in the frame so that the head of the screw can pass through the bracket and screw the bracket over the hole. Turn two screws into the wall, so that the brackets overlap them.

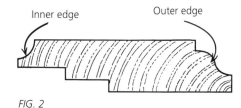

Inner edge   Outer edge

FIG. 2

Finishing and polishing

6. Sand and varnish the frame (*see* Polishing, page 19).

7. Once you have varnished the frame, have the mirror cut to measure by a glass dealer. Replace the back piece and sponge rubber. Place the mirror in its frame only after the varnish has completely dried to prevent staining it.

Mirror

Plywood   *FIG. 1*

Carcass

1. To make the frame, follow exactly the same procedure as for the top frame of the coffee table (*see* page 35). Make the joints (*see* figure 1), glue and cramp the frame together .

2. Cut rebates for the mirror and its back piece, using a router (*see* figure 1). The mirror is held in position by the back

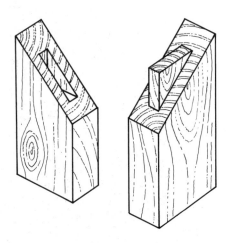

FIG. 3

Joint used in construction of frame

DOUBLE-BED BASE

A complete bed, consisting of a mattress and a base, can work out quite expensive. You could, of course, just buy a mattress and then make a base to fit. The advantage of this simple design, with the support cross-beams resting on the floor, is that shoes and slippers don't disappear under the bed!

Pine was used for the base.

Materials
2 x 1 900 mm x 230 mm x 35 mm (6 ft 3 in x 9 in x 1½ in) pieces pine for long cross-beams
2 x 1 350 mm x 230 mm x 35 mm (4 ft 5 in x 9 in x 1½ in) pieces pine for end cross-beams
11 x 1 350 mm x 150 mm x 25 mm (4 ft 5 in x 6 in x 1 in) pieces pine for slats
Woodworking adhesive
44 (45 mm/1¾ in x 10) brass countersunk screws
Sandpaper
Varnish or paint

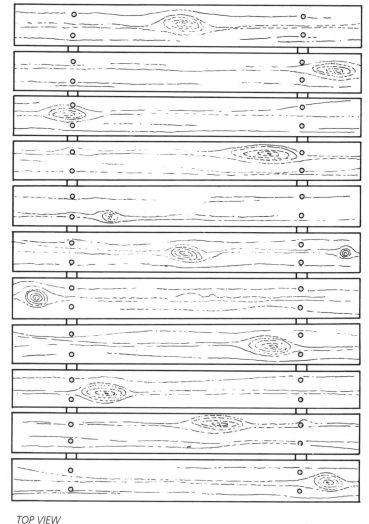

TOP VIEW

Cross-beams

1. Plane the four cross-beams on which the slats will rest to measure.

2. Mark-off the half-lapped joints (*see* Half-lapped joints, page 11).

3. Make the half-lapped joints (*see* construction without cross-beams below).

4. Glue the joints, but do not cramp.

Slats

5. Plane the slats to measure.

6. Mark-off the positions of the housings for the screws, 215 mm (8½ in) from the ends slats and 30 mm (1¼ in) from each side (*see* figure 1).

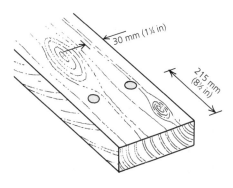

FIG. 1

7. Countersink the holes, which must be deeper than the screw heads.

8. Measure-off the position of the slats on the cross-beams. There should be a 20 mm (¾ in) space between each slat.

9. Drill pilot holes in the cross-beams, rub grease or soap on the screws to make them easier to turn in, then screw in the first slat.

10. Screw in the rest of the slats, remembering to leave a space of 20 mm (¾ in) between the slats.

Finishing and polishing

11. Sand and paint or varnish the base (*see* Polishing, page 19).

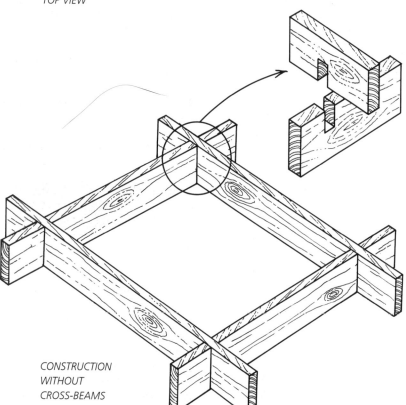

CONSTRUCTION
WITHOUT
CROSS-BEAMS

DRESSING TABLE

This piece of furniture can be used as a bureau or a traditional dressing table. There is storage space for cosmetics and/or writing materials, which are neatly tucked away when both flap tops are down.

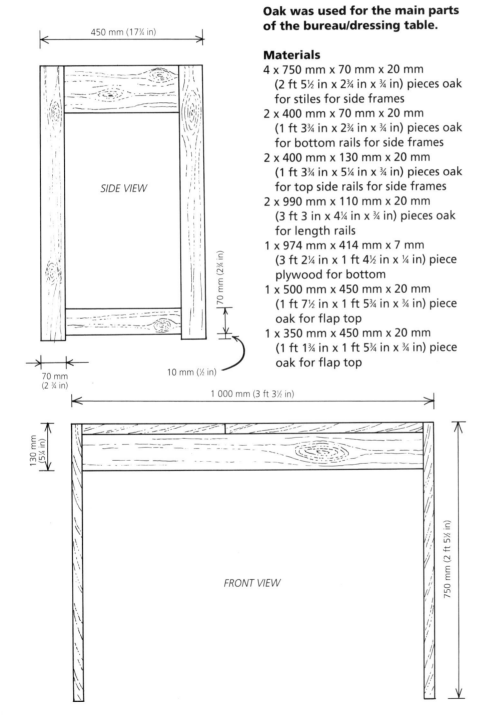

SIDE VIEW

450 mm (17¾ in)

70 mm (2¾ in)

70 mm (2 ¾ in)

10 mm (½ in)

1 000 mm (3 ft 3½ in)

130 mm (5¼ in)

750 mm (2 ft 5¼ in)

FRONT VIEW

Oak was used for the main parts of the bureau/dressing table.

Materials
4 x 750 mm x 70 mm x 20 mm
(2 ft 5½ in x 2¾ in x ¾ in) pieces oak for stiles for side frames

2 x 400 mm x 70 mm x 20 mm
(1 ft 3¾ in x 2¾ in x ¾ in) pieces oak for bottom rails for side frames

2 x 400 mm x 130 mm x 20 mm
(1 ft 3¾ in x 5¼ in x ¾ in) pieces oak for top side rails for side frames

2 x 990 mm x 110 mm x 20 mm
(3 ft 3 in x 4¼ in x ¾ in) pieces oak for length rails

1 x 974 mm x 414 mm x 7 mm
(3 ft 2¼ in x 1 ft 4½ in x ¼ in) piece plywood for bottom

1 x 500 mm x 450 mm x 20 mm
(1 ft 7½ in x 1 ft 5¾ in x ¾ in) piece oak for flap top

1 x 350 mm x 450 mm x 20 mm
(1 ft 1¾ in x 1 ft 5¾ in x ¾ in) piece oak for flap top

2 x 350 mm x 20 mm x 7 mm
(1 ft 1¾ in x ¾ in x ¼ in) plywood beams to secure flap top edges

4 x 450 mm x 25 mm x 20 mm
(1 ft 5¾ in x 1 in x ¾ in) pieces oak for flap top edges

2 x 950 mm x 10 mm x 10 mm
(3 ft 1 in x ⅜ in x ⅜ in) pieces oak for drawer runners

6 x 400 mm x 50 mm x 15 mm
(1 ft 3¾ in x 2 in x ½ in) pieces oak for drawer

1 x 400 mm x 7 mm x 7 mm
(1 ft 3¾ in x ¼ in x ¼ in) piece plywood for beam for drawer bottom

4 x 70 mm (2¾ in) brass butt hinges for flap tops

2 stays to support flap tops

1 x 500 mm x 350 mm x 7 mm
(1 ft 7½ in x 1 ft 1¾ in x ¼ in) mirror

1 bracket (to secure mirror)

Countersunk screws (20 mm/¾ in x 6) to secure hinges

30 mm (¼ in) panel pins for drawer

Woodworking adhesive

Sandpaper

Varnish

Side frames
1. Saw and plane the stiles to measure. Mark-off and chisel out the mortises for the mortise-and-tenon joints (*see* Mortise-and-tenon joints, page 12).

2. Saw and plane the rails to measure. Mark off and saw the tenons (*see* Mortise-and-tenon joints, page 12).

3. Next sand the stiles and rails for the side frames.

4. Now glue and cramp together the side frames.

5. Mark-out the slots where the length rails will fit, and chisel them out.

Length rails
6. Saw and plane the length rails to measure. Mark-off and saw the tenons.

Base
7. Plane, or use a router, to cut a groove in the length rails and side frames for the base to fit into.

8. Saw the base to measure.

Carcass
9. To assemble the carcass, first glue the length rails in the side frames around the base. The base should not be glued into the grooves.

Flap tops

10. Glue and cramp the edges of the flap tops to obtain the right size and sand until smooth.

11. Cut a groove in the edge of the flap tops, and in the two plywood beams (*see* figure 1).

FIG. 1

12. Cramp and glue the edges of the flap top.

13. Glue together the flap tops so that they fit edge-to-edge over the framework, with an allowance on the sides of 2 mm (⅛ in).

14. Fix the hinges on to the flap tops at the back, as shown in figure 2 (*see also* Hinges, page 18).

15. Secure the mirror on the larger flap top.

16. Fix stays so that the flap tops can remain in the open position when required (*see* figure 2).

FIG. 2

17. The edge of the flap tops overlap the framework by 5 mm (¼ in) and serve as a handle in the front.

Drawer

18. Make the drawer as shown in figure 3. Join the four pieces for the outer frame with corner rebates, and the

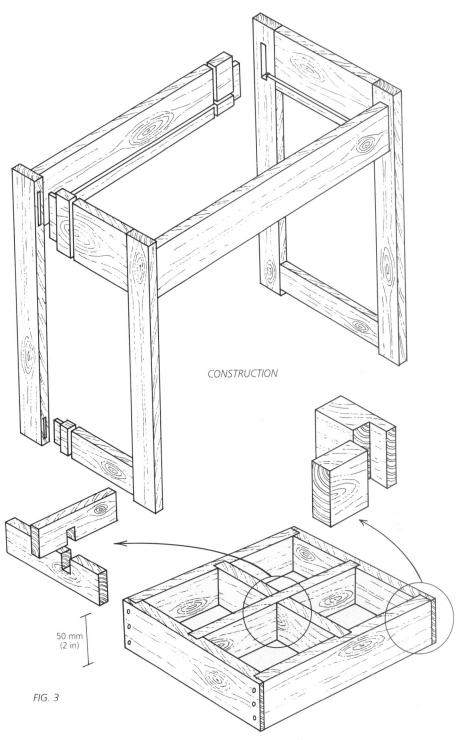

CONSTRUCTION

50 mm
(2 in)

FIG. 3

pieces that cross each other in the middle with a cross-lapped joint (*see* Cross-lapped joint, page 11). Secure the bottom of the drawer with nails or screws. The external measurements of the drawer must be 400 mm x 400 mm (1 ft 3¾ in x 1 ft 3¾ in).

19. Now fix the drawer runners. These consist of two pieces of wood secured with screws on to the inside of the length rails of the frame (so that the drawer can be moved from one side of the bureau to

the other). Make sure that there is ample space between the bottom of the drawer and the bottom of the bureau for storing cosmetics or writing materials.

Finishing and polishing

20. To finish off the construction professionally, give the bureau a final sanding with fine sandpaper (at least 120 grits).

21. Now varnish or paint the bureau depending on the finish you require (*see* Polishing, page 19)

CHILD'S BED/DESK UNIT

Children's rooms are usually small, so you have to make good use of the space available. In this unit, the bed is stacked above the desk, which is more economical than making two separate units.

Pine was used for the unit.

Materials

1 x 1 575 mm x 100 mm x 25 mm
(5 ft 2 in x 4 in x 1 in) piece pine for safety rail
4 x 1 900 mm x 100 mm x 25 mm
(6 ft 3 in x 4 in x 1 in) pieces pine for length rails
8 x 900 mm x 100 mm x 25 mm
(3 ft x 4 in x 1 in) pieces pine for cross-rails
5 x 1 780 mm x 100 mm x 25 mm
(5 ft 10½ in x 4 in x 1 in) pieces pine for uprights
4 x 425 mm x 100 mm x 25 mm
(1 ft 4¾ in x 4 in x 1 in) pieces pine for ladder rungs
4 x 1 900 mm x 20 mm x 20 mm
(6 ft 3 in x ¾ in x ¾ in) pieces pine for support strips A
4 x 900 mm x 20 mm x 20 mm
(2 ft 11½ in x ¾ in x ¾ in) pieces pine for support strips B
2 x 1 900 mm x 900 mm x 22 mm
(6 ft 3 in x 2 ft 11½ in x ¾ in) pieces blockboard for bed base board and desk top
100 (45 mm/1¾ in x 10) brass countersunk screws
40 (38 mm/1½ in x 8) countersunk screws
Woodworking adhesive
Sandpaper
Varnish
40 mm (1½ in) panel pins

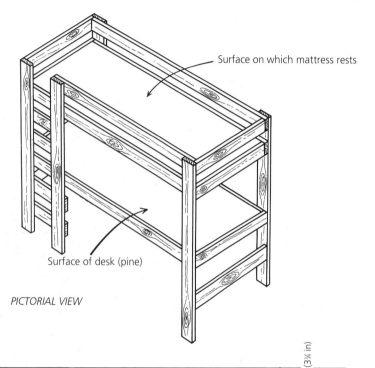

Surface on which mattress rests

Surface of desk (pine)

PICTORIAL VIEW

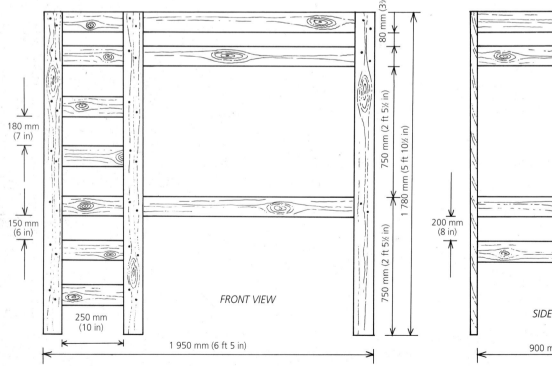

180 mm (7 in)

150 mm (6 in)

250 mm (10 in)

80 mm (3¾ in)

750 mm (2 ft 5½ in)

1 780 mm (5 ft 10½ in)

750 mm (2 ft 5½ in)

FRONT VIEW

1 950 mm (6 ft 5 in)

200 mm (8 in)

SIDE VIEW

900 mm (3 ft)

Preparation of wood

1. All the boards for the carcass (the frame for the bed and desk) must be the same width and thickness (100 mm x 25 mm/ 4 in x 1 in). Plane to measure. Sand with medium sandpaper (100 grits).

Safety rail, length rails and uprights

2. Saw the wood for the safety rail, length rails and uprights to measure.

3. Mark-off the positions where the boards will meet (*see* illustrations, page 70 for a guide).

4. Drill two holes for each position where two boards will meet on the safety rail and length rails, preferably diagonally opposite one another (*see* figure 1), and countersink the holes for the screw heads.

FIG. 1

5. Place the framework with the safety rail, length rails and uprights in position and tap a panel pin into each joint to secure temporarily to make it easier to drill pilot holes for screwing in the uprights. Do not hammer the panel pins in completely, as you must be able to remove them later. Drill the pilot holes (*see* Screws, page 18).

6. Pull the panel pins out, spread glue on each joint and turn the screws in.

7. Drill the holes where the cross-rails are attached to the safety rail, length rails and uprights, and countersink the holes.

Cross-rails

8. Saw the wood for the cross-rails to length.

9. Using panel pins, fix the cross-rails between the length frames (consisting of safety rail, length rails and uprights) so that the whole unit can stand (*see* figure 2).

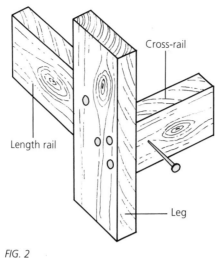

FIG. 2

10. Drill pilot holes for the screws that must be turned into the cross-rails.

11. Turn the screws in and pull out the panel pins. The frame for the bed, desk and ladder is now complete.

Support strips, bed base board and desk top

12. Fix the support strips A and B to the inside of the frame with screws (*see* figure 3). The desk top will rest on top of the support strips on the bottom part of the frame, so allow enough space above the support strips for the thickness of the desk top (*see* figure 4). The base board for the bed will rest on the support strips on the top part of the frame, so allow enough space above the support strips for the mattress (*see* figure 5).

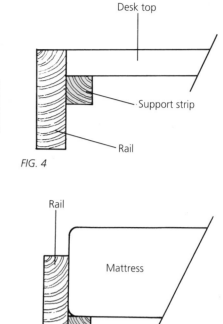

FIG. 4

FIG. 5

Ladder

13. To make the ladder, attach the rungs to the inside of the two uprights. Note that the frame for the desk top forms the third rung. Make sure that the rungs are an equal distance apart.

Finishing and polishing

14. Give the framework a final sanding with fine sandpaper (120 grits).

15. Apply varnish (*see* Polishing, page 19).

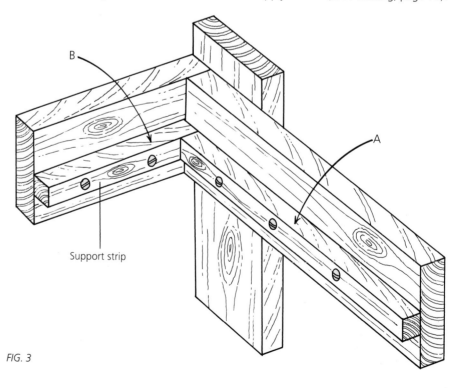

FIG. 3

BOOKRACK

With this small bookrack on your desk, you can keep your books neatly together and at hand. It is small enough not to take up much space, but large enough to hold those books which you frequently refer to.

Oak was used for this bookrack.

Materials
2 x 250 mm x 200 mm x 15 mm
   (10 in x 8 in x ½ in) pieces oak
   for sides
1 x 340 mm x 200 mm x 15 mm
   (1 ft 1½ in x 8 in x ½ in) piece oak
   for shelf
1 x 350 mm x 30 mm x 15 mm
   (1 ft 1¾ in x 1¼ in x ½ in) piece oak
   for back rail
Sandpaper
Woodworking adhesive
Varnish

Sides
1. First draw the shape of the sides on paper to fit into a 250 mm x 200 mm (10 in x 8 in) rectangle (*see* figure 1, page 74 for different shapes).

2. Saw and plane the sides to measure.

3. Transfer the shape of the sides on to the wood.

4. Saw the shape of the sides with a jig saw.

5. Mark-off the housings (*see* Housing joints, page 12) where the shelf will fit.

6. Saw and chisel out the housings or cut with a router.

CONSTRUCTION

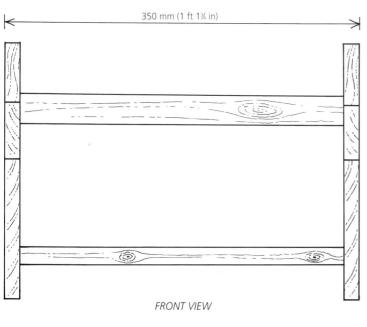

350 mm (1 ft 1¾ in)

40 mm (1½ in)

30 mm (1¼ in)

FRONT VIEW

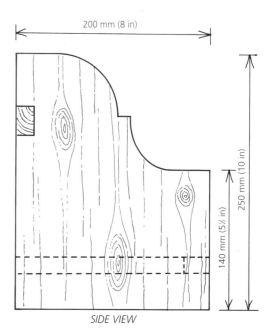

200 mm (8 in)

250 mm (10 in)

140 mm (5½ in)

SIDE VIEW

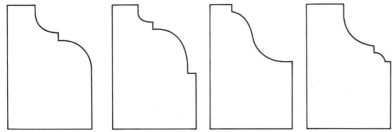

FIG. 1 *Alternative designs for sides*

Shelf

7. Saw and plane the shelf to measure.

8. Mark-out the corners so that the shelf will fit into the stopped housings.

9. Saw out the corners of the shelf.

Back rail

10. Now saw and plane the wood for the back rail to measure.

11. Mark-out the sockets at the back of the sides where the rail will fit.

12. Saw out the sockets.

Carcass

13. Sand all the parts with fine sandpaper.

14. Glue and cramp the carcass.

Finishing and polishing

15. Give the bookrack a final sanding to ensure a professional finish.

16. Varnish or paint the bookrack (*see* Polishing, page 19).

BOOKCASE

A neat bookcase not only provides space for your books but may also be used to display your most prized editions. It will look equally good in the living room, dining-room or family room. The spacing between shelves is arranged in three different heights, which should be sufficient for the whole spectrum of book sizes.

Oak was used for the bookcase.

Materials

2 x 1 200 mm x 250 mm x 20 mm (3 ft 11¼ in x 10 in x ¾ in) pieces oak for sides

4 x 1 074 mm x 250 mm x 20 mm (3 ft 6½ in x 10 in x ¾ in) pieces oak for shelves

1 x 1 074 mm x 250 mm x 20 mm (3 ft 6½ in x 10 in x ¾ in) piece oak for foot

1 x 1 086 mm x 250 mm x 20 mm (3 ft 6¾ in x 10 in x ¾ in) piece oak for top cross-rail

Woodworking adhesive

Sandpaper

Varnish or furniture oil

Sides

1. Saw and plane the sides of the bookcase to measure (*see* illustrations below for explanation).

2. Now draw the shape of the sides on paper and use tracing paper to trace it on to the wood. Saw out the shape with a jig saw or by hand with a fret saw (*see* Tools and Techniques, page 8).

3. Mark-off the position of the housings for the shelves and foot, and check thicknesses to make sure the shelves will fit into them.

4. Make the housings (*see* Housing joints, page 12).

Shelves and foot

5. Saw and plane the shelves and foot to measure.

6. Clearly mark-off the parts that must be sawn out to fit into the housings.

7. Saw out the corners (*see* Housing joints, page 12).

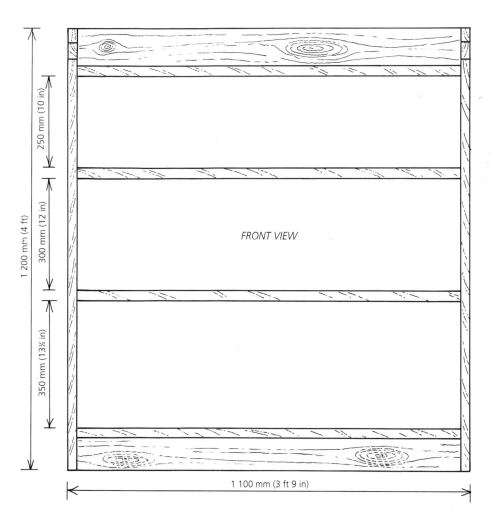

FRONT VIEW

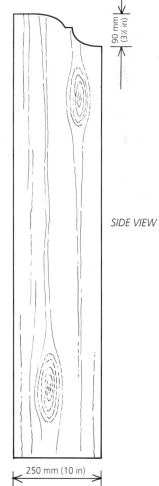

SIDE VIEW

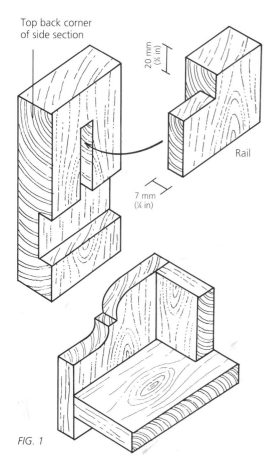

Top back corner of side section

20 mm (¾ in)

Rail

7 mm (¼ in)

FIG. 1

Top rail
8. The top rail fits into the sides by means of a bare-faced mortise-and-tenon joint (*see* figure 1). Mark-off the joint, chisel out the mortises and saw the tenons.

Carcass
9. Sand all the parts with fine sandpaper.

10. Glue and cramp the carcass (*see* Display cabinet, figure 3, page 53).

Back piece (optional)
11. The bookcase may be backed with an oak-veneered plywood back piece, but it is not necessary. If you prefer a backing, plane a rebate for it to fit into so that it will look neat and be flush with the sides of the bookcase (*see* Wall cabinet, page 42, for method).

Finishing and polishing
12. Sand the completed bookcase with fine sandpaper.

13. Varnish (see Polishing, page 19). If you decide to use oil, the bookcase will require frequent oiling. Make sure that the oil layer has dried completely before you put any books on the shelves, or the oil will stain the books.

CONSTRUCTION

FILING UNIT

This easy-to-make unit provides useful and orderly storage space for all your accounts, receipts and other documents.

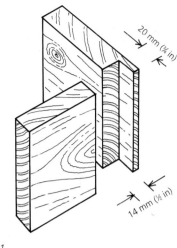

FIG. 1

Pine and hardboard were used to make the filing unit.

Materials
2 x 680 mm x 250 mm x 20 mm
  (2 ft 3 in x 10 in x ¾ in) pieces pine
  for long sides
2 x 340 mm x 250 mm x 20 mm
  (1 ft 1½ in x 10 in x ¾ in) pieces pine
  for short sides
4 x 314 mm x 250 mm x 7 mm
  (12½ in x 10 in x ¼ in) pieces hardboard for dividers
1 x 680 mm x 340 mm x 7 mm

(2 ft 3 in x 1 ft 1½ in x ¼ in) piece
hardboard for base
40 mm (1½ in) panel pins
Woodworking adhesive
Sandpaper
Varnish

Construction: frame
1. Saw and plane the sides to measure as listed above.

2. Mark-off the corner rebates for joining the sides (*see* figure 1) with a marking gauge.

3. Make the rebate (*see* figure 2), with a router.

4. Mark-off the grooves for the dividers along the long sides.

5. Now saw all the grooves using a circular saw and chisel them out with a 7 mm (¼ in) chisel.

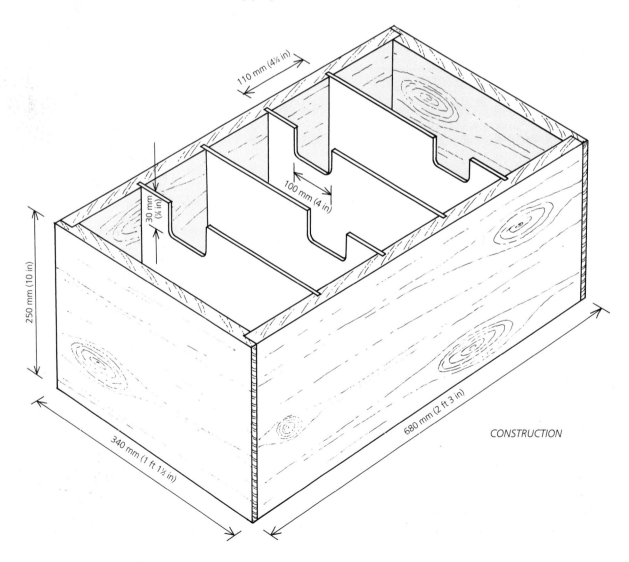

CONSTRUCTION

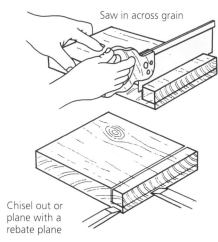

Saw in across grain

Chisel out or plane with a rebate plane

FIG. 2

Dividers

6. Saw the dividers to measure and mark off the cutouts.

7. Saw out the cutouts.

Carcass

8. Sand the sides.

9. Spread glue on the rebates in the sides and nail the unit together (*see* figure 3).

Base

10. Trace the outlines of the unit on to a piece of hardboard to determine the exact size of the base.

11. Saw out the base.

12. Spread glue on the edges of the rough side of the hardboard and nail the glued-up frame to the base.

Finishing and polishing

13. Now varnish the inside of the frame and allow to dry.

14. Slide in the dividers (varnish first if you wish).

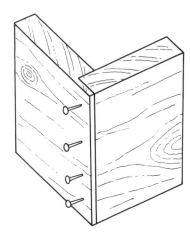

FIG. 3

15. Give the unit a final sanding (but do not sand the hardboard).

16. Varnish the completed filing unit (*see* Polishing, page 19).

SEWING CENTRE

This cabinet is a handy storage unit for a
sewing machine, fabric and threads, and has
a solid work surface for cutting and sewing.
Patterns can be stored in the drawers.

**Except where stated otherwise,
veneered chipboard was used for
this project. Match any solid wood
to the veneer of your choice.**

Materials
2 x 1 370 mm x 500 mm x 16 mm
(4 ft 6 in x 1 ft 7½ in x ½ in) pieces
veneered chipboard for sides

1 x 1 168 mm x 300 mm x 16 mm
(3 ft 9½ in x 12 in x ½ in) piece
veneered chipboard for top
3 x 1 168 mm x 480 mm x 16 mm
(3 ft 9½ in x 1 ft 6¾ in x ½ in) pieces
veneered chipboard for shelves and
bottom
3 x 500 mm x 90 mm x 16 mm
(1 ft 7½ in x 3½ in x ½ in) pieces

veneered chipboard for dividers on
either side of drawers
1 x 410 mm x 70 mm x 16 mm
(1 ft 4 in x 2¾ in x ½ in) piece
veneered chipboard for vertical
divider between doors
1 x 1 168 mm x 100 mm x 16 mm
(3 ft 9½ in x 4 in x ½ in) piece
veneered chipboard for base
2 x 510 mm x 450 mm x 16 mm
(1 ft 8 in x 1 ft 5¾ in x ½ in) pieces
veneered chipboard for sliding top
3 x 450 mm x 38 mm x 20 mm
(1 ft 5¾ in x 1½ in x ¾ in) pieces solid
wood for strips to which drawer
runners will be attached
2 x 544 mm x 90 mm x 16 mm
(1 ft 9 in x 3½ in x ½ in) pieces veneered
chipboard for false drawer faces
2 x 510 mm x 550 mm x 16 mm
(1 ft 8 in x 1 ft 9½ in x ½ in) pieces
veneered chipboard for doors
4 x 400 mm x 90 mm x 16 mm
(1 ft 3¾ in x 3½ in x ½ in) pieces

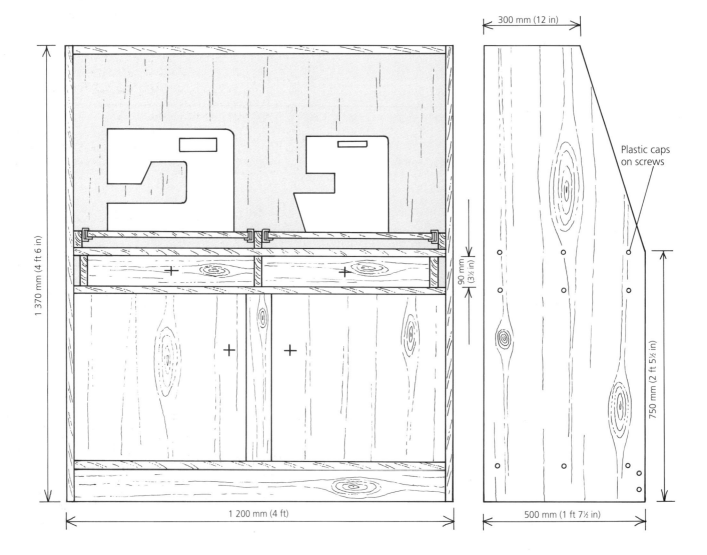

FRONT VIEW

SIDE VIEW

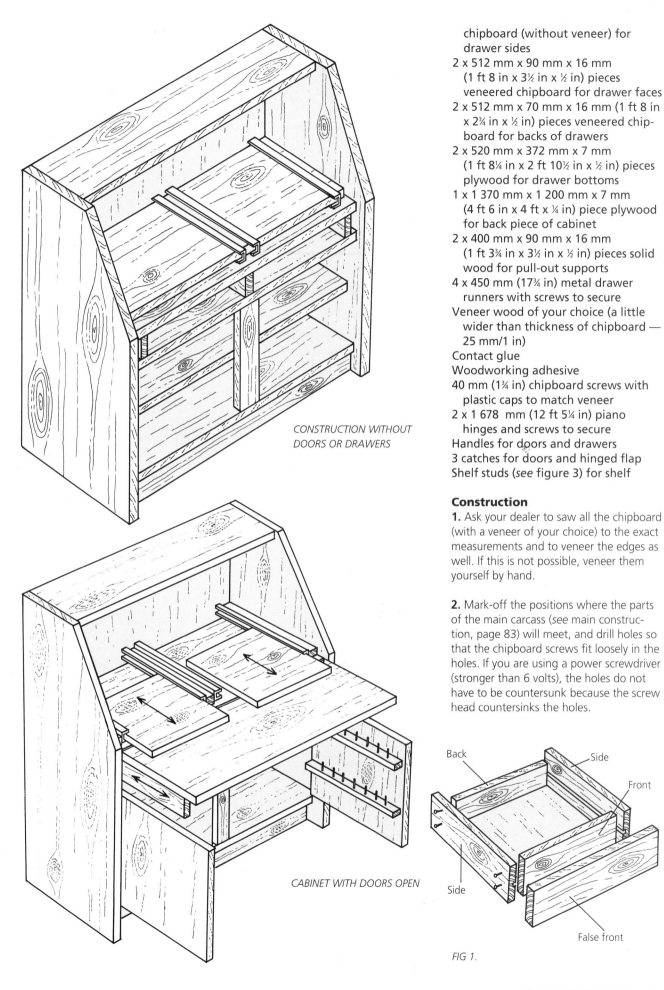

chipboard (without veneer) for
   drawer sides
2 x 512 mm x 90 mm x 16 mm
   (1 ft 8 in x 3½ in x ½ in) pieces
   veneered chipboard for drawer faces
2 x 512 mm x 70 mm x 16 mm (1 ft 8 in
   x 2¾ in x ½ in) pieces veneered chipboard for backs of drawers
2 x 520 mm x 372 mm x 7 mm
   (1 ft 8¼ in x 2 ft 10½ in x ½ in) pieces
   plywood for drawer bottoms
1 x 1 370 mm x 1 200 mm x 7 mm
   (4 ft 6 in x 4 ft x ¼ in) piece plywood
   for back piece of cabinet
2 x 400 mm x 90 mm x 16 mm
   (1 ft 3¾ in x 3½ in x ½ in) pieces solid
   wood for pull-out supports
4 x 450 mm (17¾ in) metal drawer
   runners with screws to secure
Veneer wood of your choice (a little
   wider than thickness of chipboard —
   25 mm/1 in)
Contact glue
Woodworking adhesive
40 mm (1¾ in) chipboard screws with
   plastic caps to match veneer
2 x 1 678 mm (12 ft 5¼ in) piano
   hinges and screws to secure
Handles for doors and drawers
3 catches for doors and hinged flap
Shelf studs (see figure 3) for shelf

Construction

1. Ask your dealer to saw all the chipboard
(with a veneer of your choice) to the exact
measurements and to veneer the edges as
well. If this is not possible, veneer them
yourself by hand.

2. Mark-off the positions where the parts
of the main carcass (see main construction, page 83) will meet, and drill holes so
that the chipboard screws fit loosely in the
holes. If you are using a power screwdriver
(stronger than 6 volts), the holes do not
have to be countersunk because the screw
head countersinks the holes.

*CONSTRUCTION WITHOUT
DOORS OR DRAWERS*

CABINET WITH DOORS OPEN

Back

Side

Front

Side

Side

False front

FIG 1.

3. First screw the two centre shelves, the dividers for the drawers and the pull-out supports together.

4. Now join together the two centre shelves with the top board, the bottom, the divider for the doors and the base to the sides. The shelf inside the cabinet may remain loose so that it can be adjusted if desired.

5. Screw one part of the drawer runners to the solid wooden strips. Place the runners on the inside and in the middle of the cabinet. Mark-off the space in between and saw the slip boards to measure so that they fit exactly. Screw the other part of the drawer runner to the slip boards and slide the drawers in to make sure they fit and can move in and out smoothly.

6. Saw the bottom doors to measure, taking into account the veneer on the edges (leave a clearance of about 4 mm (¼ in) for the piano hinge). First screw the hinges to the door and then to the cabinet. Fix the catches to the doors (see Catches and handles, page 19).

7. Make the drawer faces (again taking the veneer into account) to fit into the opening and complete the drawers (see figure 1, page 81 and Drawer construction, page 14).

MAIN CONSTRUCTION

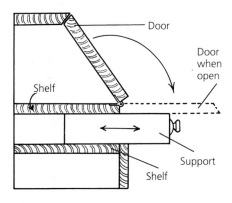

FIG. 2

8. Fit the pull-out supports. They are made of solid wood and the faces must also be veneered to make sure that the end grain is concealed.

9. Saw the top door to measure and fix the hinge. Place the door in position (see figure 2).

10. Saw the shelf that fits inside the bottom cabinet carefully to measure. Use a hammer to tap the plastic shelf stud supports into the sides of the cabinet (see figure 3). Now slide the shelf in from the back to rest on the supports.

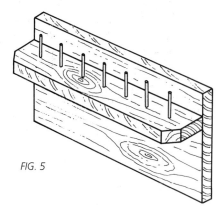

FIG. 3

11. Saw the back piece of the cabinet to measure. Drill small holes into the back and attach it to the back of the cabinet with screws. The back piece does not meet the sides of the cabinet (see illustration in figure 4).

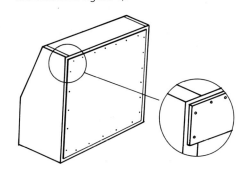

FIG. 4

12. Fix the handles to the doors, drawers and pull-out supports (see Catches and handles, page 19).

13. Attach narrow strips of wood fitted with dowels to the inside of the bottom doors with screws (see figure 5). These will be used to hold reels of thread.

FIG. 5

Finishing and polishing

14. Lightly sand the finished cabinet with fine sandpaper (about 120 grits).

15. Varnish the cabinet (see Polishing, page 19).

TOOL CHEST

Even if you are a tidy worker, you will find this chest ideal for keeping your tools close to hand at all times. Minus the inner drawers and with the addition of more decorative handles, it can be used as a linen chest.

Pine was used for the chest.

Materials
1 x 900 mm x 600 mm x 20 mm (3 ft x 1 ft 11½ in x ¾ in) piece pine for lid
2 x 900 mm x 500 mm x 20 mm (3 ft x 1 ft 7½ in x ¾ in) pieces pine for long sides
2 x 600 mm x 500 mm x 20 mm (1 ft 11½ in x 1 ft 7½ in x ¾ in) pieces pine for short sides
1 x 860 mm x 560 mm x 20 mm (2 ft 10 in x 1 ft 10 in x ¾ in) piece pine for base
2 x 940 mm x 100 mm x 20 mm (3 ft 1 in x 4 in x ¾ in) pieces pine for plinth
2 x 640 mm x 100 mm x 20 mm (2 ft 1 in x 4 in x ¾ in) pieces pine for plinth
2 x 940 mm x 40 mm x 20 mm (3 ft 1 in x 1½ in x ¾ in) pieces pine for top edge
2 x 640 mm x 40 mm x 20 mm (2 ft 1 in x 1½ in x ¾ in) pieces pine for top edge
2 x 860 mm x 20 mm x 20 mm (2 ft 10 in x ¾ in x ¾ in) pieces pine for bottom support strips
2 x 560 mm x 20 mm x 20 mm (1 ft 10 in x ¾ in x ¾ in) pieces pine for bottom support strips
6 x 860 mm x 225 mm x 20 mm (2 ft 10 in x 9 in x ¾ in) pieces pine for long sides of sliding drawers

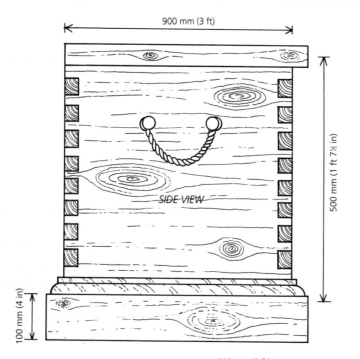

900 mm (3 ft)

500 mm (1 ft 7½ in)

100 mm (4 in)

SIDE VIEW

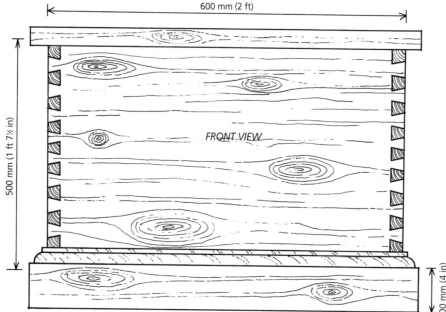

600 mm (2 ft)

500 mm (1 ft 7½ in)

100 mm (4 in)

FRONT VIEW

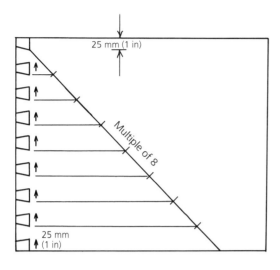

FIG. 1

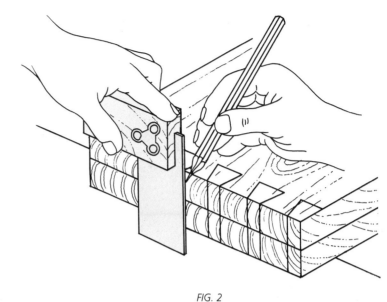

FIG. 2

6 x 200 mm x 225 mm x 20 mm
(8 in x 9 in x ¾ in) pieces pine for
short sides of sliding drawers

6 x 172 mm x 225 mm x 20 mm
(6¾ in x 9 in x ¾ in) pieces pine for
dividers for sliding drawers

3 x 832 mm x 172 mm x 9 mm
(33 in x 6 ¾ in x ⅜ in) pieces
plywood for bottoms of sliding
drawers

500 mm x 10 mm (1 ft 7½ in x ⅜ in)
thick rope for handles (or any
handles)

26 (38 mm/1½ in x no. 8) countersunk
screws

2 x 100 mm (4 in) brass butt hinges

6 (20 mm/¾ in x no. 8) countersunk
screws

Woodworking adhesive

Varnish (optional)

Glueing the sides

1. You will have to glue together pieces
of pine for the side to measure (*see* Edge
joints, page 14). Glue them a little longer
and wider than required, so that you can
saw and plane them square. Saw one
edge straight and place a try square
against it to true up the end grains, (these
can be sawn square with a jig saw). Saw
the boards to width with a circular saw.

Mark-off and saw dovetails

2. The sides are joined together by means
of dovetail joints (*see* page 13). Determine
the length of the dovetails (*see* Drawer
construction, page 15), and take the
shoulder width as 25 mm (1 in). Draw a
diagonal line (multiple of eight) to the
edge of the board and divide into eight.
Draw two dividing lines to the end grain

(parallel with the edge of the board) to
obtain the division of eight dovetails. Draw
the diagonal lines with a sliding bevel. This
procedure is explained in figure 1. It is
necessary only to mark-off the dovetails
on one end grain. This end can then be
placed over the other ends and the dovetails can then be marked with a try square
as shown in figure 2.

3. Saw and chisel out the waste wood
between the dovetails (*see* Dovetail joints,
page 13).

Mark-off and chisel out sockets

4. Trace the four sets of dovetails on to
the ends of the short sides to determine
the size of the sockets (*see* Dovetail joints,
page 13). Number the dovetails and their
corresponding sockets.

5. Saw and chisel out the sockets.
It is best to saw on the waste side of the
lines. This will ensure that the joints fit
snugly and it will not be necessary to
cramp the carcass.

Cramp and glue the carcass

6. Once all the sockets have been
removed, the joints can be tested (to
ensure that all the dovetails fit).

7. Now sand all the sides on the inside
and outside with fine sandpaper
(120 grits) to ensure a smooth finish.

8. Spread glue on one side of the joints
and tap each in with a small metal hammer and a waste block (to avoid marking
the wood). Make sure the carcass is
square and true.

9. If the joints slide in loosely and do
not remain in position on their own, you
will have to cramp them (*see* Drawer construction, page 15).

The base

10. Once the boards that make up the
base have been glued, cut the base to
measure so that it fits into the chest.

11. Wooden strips should be secured
against the inside of the box with screws
and then the base can be glued to these
strips. Spread glue on the strips and
stack weights on the bottom as
shown in figure 3.

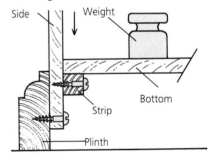

FIG. 3

Plinth

12. Saw the pine for the plinth to measure,
and shape the edges using a router. It
must project a thickness of 20 mm/¾ in
(equal to the thickness of a piece of pine)
beyond each end of the chest.

Saw these ends off at an angle of 45°
(*see* figure 4, page 86). Make sure that
all four parts of the plinth's end grains
are sawn in this way, and then glued-up
and secured to the chest with screws (*see*
figure 3 for clarification).

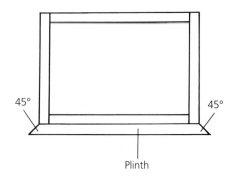

FIG. 4

45°　　　　　45°

Plinth

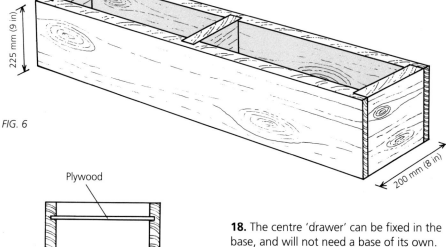

FIG. 6

225 mm (9 in)

200 mm (8 in)

Lid

13. Saw the glued-up lid to measure so that the outer edge is level with the outside of the chest.

14. Fit a moulding as follows along the edge of the lid (face and sides) to finish it off neatly and prevent it from warping (*see* figure 5). Plane a groove into the end grain side of the lid (using a plough plane or router), and then glue the moulding with a piece of plywood that fits into the grooves in the lid and mouldings (*see* figure 5).

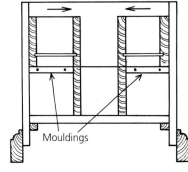

Plywood

FIG. 7

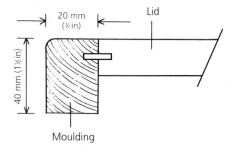

20 mm (¾ in)

Lid

40 mm (1½ in)

Moulding

FIG. 5

15. Fix the lid to the chest with two butt hinges (see Hinges, page 18). The carcass of the chest is now complete.

16. Two holes can be drilled into the sides of the chest and thick plaited rope threaded through it to serve as handles. Knot the ropes on the inside. Alternatively, attach handles of your choice.

Sliding drawers

17. Make three drawers (or boxes) for extra storage space inside the box. The dividers may be adjusted as you feel necessary. Figure 6 shows clearly how these drawers are constructed. The drawers have corner rebates on the corners and common housing joints in the centre (*see* explanation under Drawer construction, page 15). The plywood base fits into a rebate which is planed on the inside (*see* figure 7).

Mouldings

FIG. 8

18. The centre 'drawer' can be fixed in the base, and will not need a base of its own. The two side drawers rest loosely on mouldings attached to the side of the chest with screws so that they can be moved out of the way to make use of the space below (*see* figures 8 and 9).

Finishing and polishing

19. Give the chest a final sanding, and varnish if you wish (*see* Polishing, page 19).

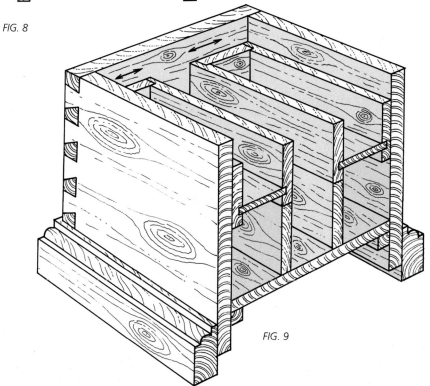

FIG. 9

CARPENTER'S WORKBENCH

A good workbench is essential for any woodworker who intends doing 'professional' work, and wants to enjoy doing it! It allows you to cramp wood properly when you saw, plane or chisel, and especially when you use power tools. It is also safer to work on a workbench.

Pine and plywood were used for this project.

Materials

4 x 778 mm x 76 mm x 50 mm
(2 ft 6¾ in x 3 in x 2 in) pieces of pine for stiles of side frame

4 x 700 mm x 76 mm x 50 mm
(2 ft 3½ in x 3 in x 2 in) pieces of pine for rails of side frames

4 x 880 mm x 76 mm x 50 mm
(2 ft 10¾ in x 3 in x 2 in) pieces of pine for length rails

2 x 558 mm x 76 mm x 50 mm
(1 ft 10 in x 3 in x 2 in) pieces of pine for dividers

2 x 718 mm x 468 mm x 9 mm
(2 ft 4¼ in x 1 ft 6½ in x ⅜ in) pieces of plywood for side frames

1 x 558 mm x 468 mm x 9 mm

CONSTRUCTION

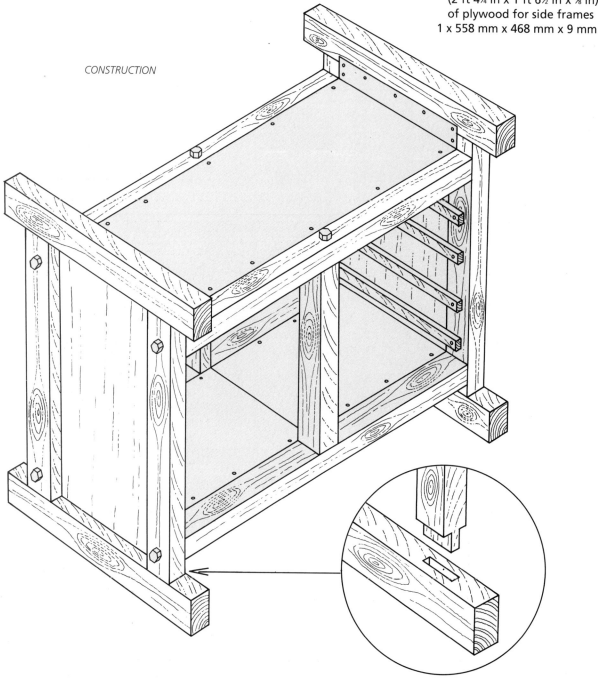

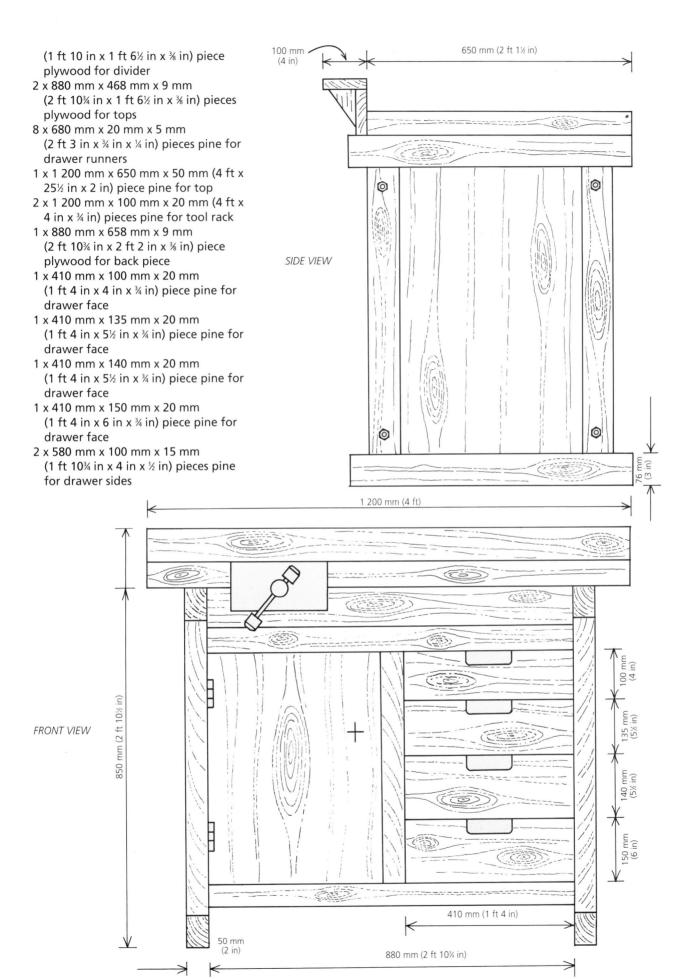

(1 ft 10 in x 1 ft 6½ in x ⅜ in) piece plywood for divider

2 x 880 mm x 468 mm x 9 mm (2 ft 10¾ in x 1 ft 6½ in x ⅜ in) pieces plywood for tops

8 x 680 mm x 20 mm x 5 mm (2 ft 3 in x ¾ in x ¼ in) pieces pine for drawer runners

1 x 1 200 mm x 650 mm x 50 mm (4 ft x 25½ in x 2 in) piece pine for top

2 x 1 200 mm x 100 mm x 20 mm (4 ft x 4 in x ¾ in) pieces pine for tool rack

1 x 880 mm x 658 mm x 9 mm (2 ft 10¾ in x 2 ft 2 in x ⅜ in) piece plywood for back piece

1 x 410 mm x 100 mm x 20 mm (1 ft 4 in x 4 in x ¾ in) piece pine for drawer face

1 x 410 mm x 135 mm x 20 mm (1 ft 4 in x 5½ in x ¾ in) piece pine for drawer face

1 x 410 mm x 140 mm x 20 mm (1 ft 4 in x 5½ in x ¾ in) piece pine for drawer face

1 x 410 mm x 150 mm x 20 mm (1 ft 4 in x 6 in x ¾ in) piece pine for drawer face

2 x 580 mm x 100 mm x 15 mm (1 ft 10¾ in x 4 in x ½ in) pieces pine for drawer sides

100 mm (4 in)

650 mm (2 ft 1½ in)

SIDE VIEW

76 mm (3 in)

1 200 mm (4 ft)

FRONT VIEW

850 mm (2 ft 10½ in)

100 mm (4 in)

135 mm (5½ in)

140 mm (5½ in)

150 mm (6 in)

410 mm (1 ft 4 in)

50 mm (2 in)

880 mm (2 ft 10¾ in)

2 x 580 mm x 135 mm x 15 mm
(1 ft 10¾ in x 5½ in x ½ in) pieces pine
for drawer sides
2 x 580 mm x 140 mm x 15 mm
(1 ft 10¾ in x 5½ in x ½ in) pieces pine
for drawer sides
2 x 580 mm x 150 mm x 15 mm
(1 ft 10¾ in x 6 in x ½ in) pieces pine
for drawer sides
1 x 410 mm x 80 mm x 15 mm
(1 ft 4 in x 3¾ in x ½ in) piece pine for
drawer back piece
1 x 410 mm x 115 mm x 15 mm
(1 ft 4 in x 4½ in x ½ in) piece pine for
drawer back piece
1 x 410 mm x 120 mm x 15 mm
(1 ft 4 in x 4¾ in x ½ in) piece pine
for drawer back piece
1 x 410 mm x 130 mm x 15 mm
(1 ft 4 in x 5¼ in x ½ in) piece pine for
drawer back piece
4 x 388 mm x 566 mm x 7 mm
(1 ft 3¼ in x 1 ft 10¼ in x ¼ in) pieces
pine for drawer bases
1 x 530 mm x 420 mm x 16 mm
(1 ft 8¾ in x 1 ft 4½ in x ½ in) piece
veneered chipboard for door
1 bench vice
4 x 70 mm x 10 mm (3 in x ⅜ in) bolts
and nuts to secure vice
1 x 230 mm x 100 mm x 50 mm
(9 in x 4 in x 2 in) piece pine for
spacer for securing bench vice.
(The size will vary according to the
size of the bench vice.)
2 bench vice hooks (size must
correspond with vice)
16 x 100 mm (4 in) lag screws to
assemble carcass
Woodworking adhesive
Varnish or paint

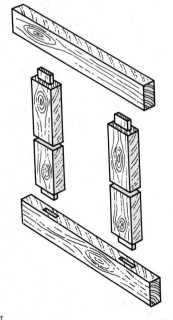

FIG. 1

Side frames

1. Saw and plane the wood for the side frames (stiles and rails) to measure.

2. Mark-off the mortises and tenons as indicated in figure 1.

3. Chisel the mortises and saw the tenons (*see* Mortise-and-tenon joints, page 12).

4. Glue and cramp the frames.

5. Using a router, cut a rebate, the depth of the plywood, to fit the side panels (*see* figure 2).

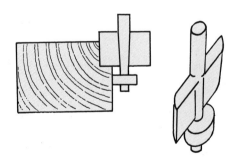

FIG. 2

6. Cut the plywood panels to measure so that they fit into the rebate, and secure them with glue and panel pins.

7. Plane and saw the length rails to measure and plane a rebate on the inside of all four rails (*see* figure 3 for the bit used in the router).

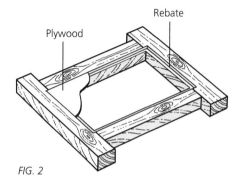

FIG. 3

8. Cut the two pieces of plywood to measure, so that they fit between the length rails to form the tops.

9. Secure the plywood between the length rails with glue and panel pins.

10. Saw and plane dividers to measure and plane their rebates.

11. Saw plywood for the divider frames to measure and secure between dividers with glue and panel pins.

12. Mark-off the position of the lag screws and drill holes. Drill pilot holes (*see* figure 4) for the bolts. Pass the bolt loosely through the first section and turn it into a pilot hole up to two-thirds the thickness of the shank of the nut.

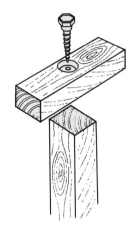

FIG. 4

13. Next, assemble the carcass with lag screws.

14. Mark-off the height of the drawers as shown in the illustration of the carcass on page 88 and determine the middle of each drawer's height.

15. Plane the drawer runners to measure and space over the centre line as determined in step 14. Turn the screws so that the drawers can slide in more easily.

Top

16. Glue the top pieces together (*see* Edge joints, page 14).

17. Secure the top with lag screws, working from the top into the upper cross-rails of the side frames. Countersink the screw heads in the top (*see* figure 5).

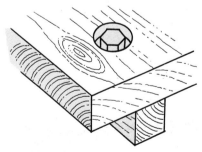

FIG. 5

Back of workbench

18. The back piece consists of plywood which is screwed into or nailed to the upper and lower sides of the length rails. At the sides it is secured to the back of the side frames (*see* figure 6).

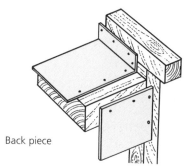

Back piece

FIG. 6

Door

19. The door consists of a piece of veneered chipboard which is cut to measure and the edges finished with veneer. Plane the door to measure, veneer the edges and hang the door (*see* Hinges, page 18).

20. Fix a catch and a handle in position (*see* Catches and handles, page 19).

Drawers

21. Plane and saw the wood for the drawers to measure and make them (*see* Drawer construction, page 14).

22. Glue and cramp the drawers.

23. Plane rebates into the sides of each drawer so that they can slide on runners (*see* Hall table, page 28).

24. Mark-off and cut out sections of the drawer faces to serve as handles (*see* illustration of the front view, page 89). Use other kinds of handles if you wish.

Securing the bench vice

25. Cut a notch in the top to fit one bench hook (*see* figure 7).

26. Saw a block of wood to measure to fit between the vice and the top of the workbench, so that the hooks of the vice lie level with the top of the workbench (*see* figure 8).

FIG. 7

27. Use bolts to secure the vice to the top (*see* figure 7).

Tool rack

28. The tool rack consists of two planks joined together and then attached to the back of the workbench with screws. The horizontal plank has cut outs to hold chisels, screwdrivers, a try square, marking gauge, files and rasps (*see* figure 9). Drill the holes and square-off with a chisel where necessary. Make up the rack and attach it to the workbench with screws. Triangular or rectangular blocks can be fixed between the two boards with screws to reinforce them (*see* figure 10).

Finishing and polishing

29. Even a functional item like this should be properly sanded. Apply a few layers of varnish to protect your workbench (*see* Polishing, page 19).

Screw together

FIG. 10

Top of workbench

Wooden block

FIG. 8

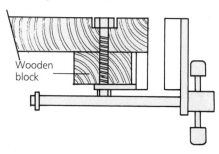

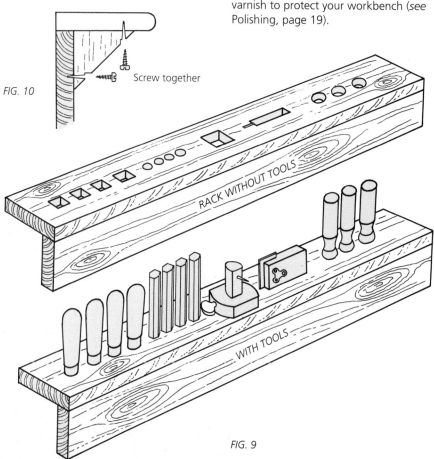

RACK WITHOUT TOOLS

WITH TOOLS

FIG. 9

LIST OF SUPPLIERS

UNITED KINGDOM

B & Q plc
Portswood House
Hampshire Corporate Park
Chandlers Ford
Eastleigh
Hants SO5 3YX
Tel: (01703) 256256
(Branches throughout the UK)

Do-It-All
Falcon House
The Minories
Dudley
West Midlands DY2 8PG
Tel: (01384) 456456
(Branches throughout the UK)

Texas Homecare
Homecharm House
Parkfarm
Wellingborough
Northampton
Tel: (01933) 679679
(Branches throughout the UK)

Travis Perkins
Lodge Way House
Lodge Way
Harlestone Road
Northampton
NN5 7UG
Tel: (01604) 752424
(Branches throughout the UK)

Wickes
120-138 Station Road
Harrow
Middlesex HA1 2QB
Tel: (0181) 863 5696
(Branches throughout the UK)

Homebase Ltd
Beddington House
Wallington
Surrey
Tel: (0181) 784 7200
(Branches throughout the UK)

Harcross Timber and Building Supplies
1 Great Tower Street
London EC3R 5AH
Tel: (0171) 711 1444

Great Mills Retail
RNC House
Paulton
Bristol BS18 5SX
Tel: (01761) 416034
(Branches throughout the UK)

Jewson Ltd
Intwood Road
Cringleford
Norwich NR4 UXB
Tel: (01603) 56133
(Branches throughout the UK)

AUSTRALIA

Mitre 10 (NSW) Ltd
122 Newton Road
Wetherill Park NSW 2164
Tel: (02) 725 3222
(Branches throughout Australia)

BBC Hardware Stores (Head Office)
P O Box 201
Parramatta 2124
Tel: (02) 683 888
(Branches throughout Australia)

NEW ZEALAND

Carter Holt Builders Supplies
Head office: Tel: (09) 849 4153
(Branches throughout Auckland)

Placemakers
Head office: Tel: (09) 303 0299
(Branches throughout New Zealand)

The Building Depot
Head office: Tel: (09) 827 0905
(Branches throughout Auckland)

Exotic Building Supplies
Head office: Tel: (09) 274 5755
(Branches throughout Auckland)

Benchmark Building Supplies
Head office: Tel: (09) 815 1506
(Branches throughout New Zealand)

GLOSSARY

Blockboard A board product made from strips of solid pine that are glued at the sides, with plywood top and bottom (also called lumberboard).

Beading A strip of wood used to attach glass or woodpanels to a construction. A beading is also a shaped strip of wood used to decorate a piece of furniture. (*see also* Crown moulding)

Butt joint Method of joining the edges of two boards laterally (*see also* Edge joints).

Carcass The main construction of a table or cabinet without drawers or doors.

Chipboard A wood board product made from wood chips mixed with glue and pressed under high pressure.

Contact adhesive Glue that does not need to be cramped in order to bond. A layer of glue is applied to each surface, allowed to dry until tacky and then pressed together.

Cross-lapped joint *See* Half-lapped joints.

Cross-cut To saw across the grain. (*see* Rip)

Crown moulding A shaped piece of wood that is glued or mounted on the top of a cabinet or shelf to decorate it.

Double-point gauge Tool used to measure off mortises and tenons for joints (also called mortise-and-tenon gauge).

Dovetail joints A secure method of joining two pieces of wood placed side by side. Used primarily for the construction of drawers and cabinets.

Dry cramp Assemble under pressure without gluing to check if all parts fit and are true.

Edge joints When planks are glued along the edges and joined to form a greater surface area, for example, a table top. (Also known as butt joints or rubbed joints).

Grain The stripes or veins on the surface of wood visible when growth rings are cut through. The grain dictates the direction in which the wood should be planed.

Grit The measure of coarseness of sand-paper. The higher the grit, the finer the sandpaper.

Groove A trough or channel which is made in wood – either with the grain or across the grain.

Grooved joints A groove is cut across the grain to house the edge of another plank, so forming a joint (*see* Housing).

Half-lapped joints This joint is used to connect two pieces of wood that intersect perpendicularly. While more simple to construct than mortise-and-tenons, dovetails or housings, they are not as strong as the more complex joints. Variations include cross-lapped and end-lapped joints.

Hardboard A board made from wood-fibres that are pressed together at high pressure without gluing.

Housing A slot or recess made in a piece of timber in order to accommodate the end of another board.

Kerf(s) A score made across the wood grain with a sharp point or chisel. Used to mark-off a saw line.

Melamine A thin, hard plastic layer which is usually laminated onto chipboard.

Mirrors When securing mirrors in a construction (page 69, fig.2) corner-brackets are used.

Mitre A joint in which the two connect-ing pieces of wood are sawed or planed usually at an angle of 45°, so forming a 90° angle.

Mortise A rectangular hole made in a piece of wood to fit a tenon, forming a mortise-and-tenon joint.

Panel A glass, plywood or solid wood sheet on the inside of a frame.

Pilot hole A hole made with a small drill bit to determine the direction of a larger bit used later.

Plinth The base of a cabinet fitting under the carcass to form the foot-piece.

Plywood A sheet of laminated wood consisting of three or more layers of thin solid wood glued together. The grain of each consecutive layer is at 90° to that of the previous layer.

Rail The horizontal section of a door-frame, or the wooden piece between the legs of a table, or the sides of a cabinet.

Rebate An L-shaped groove made at the edge of a piece of wood usually to house the end of another plank.

Rip To saw a plank along its length with the grain. (*see also* Cross-cut)

Sawing list A list of dimensions which is required for a particular project.

Scraper A sharp-edged tool which is used to remove paint or chisel out wood across the grain.

Screw sizes Screws are measured by both length and by a standard measure (which is a figure used internationally to identify the size of screws).

Skew-nail A method of driving nails into wood at an angle in order to strengthen a joint.

Stiles The vertical sections of a doorframe.

Stopped (Blind) A tenon or groove that does not stretch across the entire width of a plank. (*see* Tenon)

Tenon The end of a plank which is reduced to ⅓ of its thickness thereby forming a tongue which fits snugly into a hole (or mortise) in another plank. The finished joint is known as a mortise-and-tenon joint.

Veneer A thin layer of solid wood or sometimes an artificial surface. Chipboard is often covered with veneer to give a specific wood finish.

FURTHER READING

Blandford, Percy, *Practical Carpentry*,
Macdonald & Company, London, 1985

De Cristoforo, R.J., *The Magic of your Radial Arm Saw*,
Reston Publishing Company, Virginia, 1980

Hontoir, Anthony, *The Practical Woodwork Book*,
John Murray, London, 1986

Jackson, Albert and Day, David, *Collins Complete Woodworkers Manual*, Harpers Collins Publishers, 1992

Jackson, Albert and Day, David, *The Complete Book of Tools*,
Michael Joseph Limited, London, 1978

Lawrence, Mike, *Step-by-Step Outdoor Woodwork*,
New Holland Publishers, London,1993

Martensson, Alf, *Basic Woodworking*,
Treasure Press, London, 1986

Pettite, Tom, *Woodwork Made Easy*,
W.H. Allen and Company, London, 1980

Stokes, Gordon, *Machine and Power Tools for Woodwork*,
Bell & Hyman, 1986

Walton, John, *Woodwork in Theory and Practice*,
Australian Publishing Company, Hornsby, 1978,

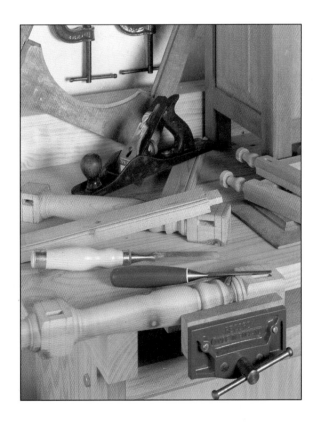

B
band saw 9, 10
bathroom cabinet 57-9
belt sander 8, 9
bench saw 8
bench vice 7, 8
bookcase 75-7
bookrack 73-4
bottle rack 51
brackets (wall) 42, 58
butt joint (*see* edge joints)

C
C-clamps 8
cabinet saw (*see* circular saw)
carpenter's workbench 88-92
catches 19
centre drill bit 7, 8
child's bed/desk unit 70-2
chipboard 11
chisel 7, 8, 18
circular saw 9, 10
cocktail cabinet/serving trolley 47-51
coffee table 34-6
common mortise-and-tenon joint 12-3
construction methods 15-7
corner dovetail joint 13-4
countersink bit 7, 8
cross-lapped joint 11
crown moulding 24, 41
cutting board 55-6

D
dimensions (of wood) 11
dining-room table 44-6
display cabinet 52-4
door construction (for a cabinet) 16-7
doorknobs 19
double-bed base 65-6
double-point gauge (*see* mortise-and-tenon gauge)
dovetail joints
    corner 13-4
    drawer 14
dovetail plate 8
drawer construction 15-6
drawer dovetail joint 14
dressing table 67-9
drill bits 8
drill press 10

E
edge joints 14
end-lapped joint 11-2

F
filing unit 78-9
finishing 19
firmer chisel 7, 8

G
G-cramp 7, 8
gouging tool 17
grooved joint (*see* housing joints)

H
half-lapped joints
    cross-lapped 11
    end-lapped 11-2
hall stand 22-4
hall table with drawers 26-8
halving joint (*see* half-lapped joints)
hammer 7, 8
hand tools 7
hand-held power tools 8-9
handles 19
hardwood 11
haunched mortise-and-tenon joint 13
hinges 18-9
housing joints 12

J
jack plane 7, 8
jig saw 8, 8-9
joints 11-4
    dovetail 13-4
    edge 14
    half-lapped 11-2
    housing 12
    mortise-and-tenon 12-3
    tools for measuring 8
    tools for shaping 8

K
key rack 20-1

L
lathe 9, 10

M
machine tools 9-10
magazine rack 32-3
magnetic catch 19
mallet 7, 8
marking gauge 8
melamine 11
mirror frame 63-4
mortise chisel 7, 8
mortise-and-tenon gauge 7, 8
mortise-and-tenon joints
    common 12-3
    haunched 13
music centre cabinet 37-9

N
nail punch 7, 8
nails 18

O
oil polish 19
orbital sander 8, 9

P
panel saw (*see* tenon saw)
paring tool 17
pencil compass 8
panel pins 15, 18
planes 7, 8, 10
planed wood 11

plough plane 7, 8
plywood 11
polishing 19
polyurethane varnish 19
power drill 8
power tools, hand-held 8-9

R
radial saw (*see* circular saw)
rebate plane 7, 8
roller catch 19
round-nosed scraper 18
router 8, 9
ruler 8

S
sanding drums 9
sandpaper 19
sash cramp 7, 8
saws 7, 8, 9, 10
sawing list, drawing up a 11
screws 18
serving trolley (*see* cocktail cabinet)
sewing centre 80-3
single-point gauge 7, 8
skew chisel 18
sliding bevel 7, 8
spring catch 19
staining 19
surface planer 10

T
T-bar cramps 8
tape measure 7, 8
telephone table 29-31
tenon saw 7
thicknesser 10
tool chest 84-7
tools 8
tools, woodturning 17-8
towel rack 60-2
try square 7, 8
turning (a table leg) 17
turning wood 17-8
twist drill bit 7

U
unplaned wood 11

V
varnish 19

W
wall brackets 42, 58
wall cabinet 40-3
wood
    planed 11
    purchasing 11
    staining 19
    tools for preparation 8
    turning 17-8
    unplaned 11
woodturning tools 17-8
workbench 8